WHAT OTHERS ARE SAYING

This is the story of heroic men who had no idea they were performing as heroes.

Angela's book opens doors about relationships and information that many citizens of our country never knew took place. It's a book that is enlightening and that presents outstanding accomplishments by inexperienced young men to whom a soldier's failure was not an option. A heartfelt, poignant read that makes one proud to be a United States citizen.

—**Dr. Vera J. Wall**

Phantom Seven is the amazing story of the OSS from the viewpoints of six of its original members—ordinary people who led extraordinary lives during their tours of duty. The OSS was the forerunner to the C.I.A., and its members are still honored today by the Agency.

I had the honor of having Benny McCoy speak to one of my university political science classes to tell us his fascinating experiences, of which hardly anyone is aware. It is definitely time for The Phantom Seven to make themselves known and claim their rightful place in history.

—**Cissie J. Owen**
Retired C.I.A. and Adjunct Instructor, Lamar University

In his bestselling book, Tom Brokaw unveils what he calls the "Greatest Generation." They didn't have state-of-the-art everything, but they were able to build America into the greatest of nations. These people were united by a common cause and values. They were men and women who had loyalty, determination, grit, and integrity that far overshadowed any of their deficiencies, doubts, or fears.

B. H. McCoy is a man who embodies those great qualities that are characteristic of his generation. He also possesses qualities that even set him apart from his great generation. His intellect and his ability to remain steady under pressure made him a natural candidate for the OSS.

—**Reverend Terry Pugh**
First United Pentecostal Church, Odessa, Texas

Those who work faithfully behind the scenes are as great as leaders like Churchill, Eisenhower, Roosevelt, and Truman are great. Though unseen and unknown until now, my dear friend Benny McCoy and the Phantom Seven are now revealed as the true heroes they have secretly been. The Holy Scripture says it is required in stewards that a man be found faithful. Well done, Phantom Seven.

—**Reverend V. Arlen Guidroz** Pastor of The Life Church, Dallas, Texas

PHANTOM SEVEN

Secret Heroes of WWII and OSS

PHANTOM SEVEN
Secret Heroes of WWII and OSS

ANGELA HORN

JoyLife Press

JoyLife Press (P.O. Box 956, Huntington, TX 75949) functions only as book publisher. As such, the ultimate design, content, editorial accuracy, and views expressed or implied in this work are those of the author.

All Scripture verses are taken from the *King James Version* of the Bible.

ISBN-13: **978-0692248829** Custom Universal
ISBN-10: **069224882X**
Library of Congress Catalog Card Number: 2009909158

To my inspiring and wonderful dad, Rev. B. H. McCoy, who reminded me that I can do anything I set my mind to, who loved my mother and our family exceptionally, and who I especially dedicate *Phantom Seven* to.

To my late, beloved, and elegant mother, Archie Myrl Morehead McCoy, who loved my dad and her children unconditionally, inspired me with her artistic talent, and helped me to write the Home Front chapter.

To my late, beloved, and delightful mother-in-law, Fern Beaushaw Horn, who loved and treated me like a daughter and helped me to write the Home Front chapter.

To the Phantom Seven and their spouses, both the survivors and those who have gone on to the other side, who have set an amazing example of love that lasts for a lifetime.

CONTENTS

&

ACKNOWLEDGMENTS

න

PHANTOM SEVEN BECAME a reality because of the help of many to whom I give thanks:

> My help cometh from the Lord, which made heaven and earth.
> —Psalm 121:2

Greg, my handsome and fun husband, I am grateful for your faithful support throughout the writing of *Phantom Seven*.

Chrissie, thank you, my beautiful daughter, for running errands, scanning photos, and especially for taking that gorgeous picture of Nana's locket.

Daddy, I always love to listen to your stories! Thank you for all that you contributed to *Phantom Seven*. I appreciate you for your faithful love and loyalty to our family, country, and God.

Thank you, Francis, Hans, LaVerne, and Lloyd for sharing your WWII and OSS stories with me. I appreciate all of your contributions to *Phantom Seven*, including your participation in the Brownsville meeting.

Pastor Gerald Nilsen, thank you for inviting Greg, Chrissie, and me to minister to your church family and for telling me about Arne Nilsen's World War II experiences in Norway. Thank you for opening the door of opportunity to include Arne's story in *Phantom Seven*.

Arne Nilsen, thank you for sharing your underground experiences from World War II with me and for graciously allowing me to include them in *Phantom Seven*.

Randall, thank you for helping your sis' by being my faithful reader and sharing your ideas. I appreciate all the time you devoted to *Phantom Seven*.

Darrell, thank you for assisting your sis' with the Brownsville group meeting and with the naming of *Phantom Seven*.

Sherry, my sis-in-law with the beautiful smile, thank you for cheering me on in my *Phantom Seven* journey and for the encouraging texts.

Shara, my sweet niece who always smiles, thank you for coming to my rescue! I am grateful for your help in sending photos.

Linda, my sis-in-law with the beautiful laugh, thank you for coming to my rescue! I appreciate your help in sending photos.

i

Penny Daigle, you spent much time in helping me to prepare for *Phantom Seven* by listening to Dad's sermon tapes and typing for me. Thank you!

Louise Burkhartsmeier, I appreciate your generosity in taking the time and effort to visit the Lido building in Paris, France, where my dad and his OSS cohorts worked during WWII. Thank you for giving me the photos to include in *Phantom Seven*.

Jenny Margotta, thank you for your help in formatting the manuscript and book cover this this second printing of *Phantom Seven*.

Especially to my husband, daughters, father, brothers, and to every other member of my family, relatives, and friends, thank you for loving me, making me laugh, encouraging me, and participating in the title name voting.

I want to thank all of the *Phantom Seven* investors for their contributions and support.

To my *Phantom Seven* readers, thank you for your interest. I thought of you all along this journey because I wanted you to see a glimpse of how this group in *Phantom Seven* made a difference in World War II.

FOREWORD

ℰℐ

WHEN THE JAPANESE attacked Pearl Harbor, America was a reluctant sleeping giant. She awakened from her stupor to join the rest of the world in its fight for freedom against tyranny. People's lives were suddenly changed. Individual aspirations and dreams were put on hold for the sake of country. The call went forth for every able-bodied American man and woman to make personal sacrifices. Some were called to work in factories at home; others went off to fight the enemy on foreign soil.

Like a multifaceted diamond, every war is full of personal accounts that have been lived out by the brave and daring. Angela McCoy Horn brings to light a facet of the war many don't know about. Angela grew up admiring her father for being a man of God with a high regard for family, truth, and honor. What she didn't know about was her father's unique role in the Second World War. Her discovery came in bits and pieces, not because her father didn't want to share, but because he was sworn to secrecy by an oath he considered sacred. When the time was right, B.H. McCoy began to share tidbits of the secret he had held inside for so many years; he was handpicked to be part of a very select group of men called the OSS. *Phantom Seven* is a compilation of interviews Angela had with her father and six other men, five of whom served with him on this highly specialized team.

All former OSS agents had one thing in common: they all could type. In a day when it was not so common for a man to have mastered this talent, they stood out among their peers. Their fate was sealed early on, and after boot camp and additional training, they were eventually assigned to an elite fraternity of men who served their country by acting as cryptographers.

Each agent has his own story to tell that weaves together these men's fascinating journeys from enlistment, language schools, and ocean voyages, to fearful nights of air raids and being bombed, to seeing fascinating world leaders, movie stars, and entertainers along their journeys. History reveals that the effectiveness of the OSS during World War II most likely shaved more than a year off of the war. Passing top-secret messages from field agents, resistance fighters, and spies on to General "Ike" Eisenhower, Winston

Churchill, and General George Marshall in Washington, D.C., was very vital to the Allies' victory over the Axis Powers.

If you have an interest in World War II, you undoubtedly will enjoy reading this book.

—**John Wolfram**
Former UDT/SEAL Vietnam Veteran
Apollo 11 rescue swimmer

PREFACE

ℬ

CHILDREN MAY HEAR their parents' stories of the "good old days" told repeatedly. And after their parents are gone, those stories become memories to pass down to future generations as treasures. Lest those treasures be forgotten, someone must take the baton and pass it to younger generations. This book is written as my baton to the younger generations in my family and to those in your family.

When I was in the seventh grade, history was my favorite class. The teacher's enthusiasm made history come alive for me. Extra credit, which I often took advantage of, was given to any student who recited quotes of famous people in history in front of the class. Twenty-five years before I sat in my seventh-grade history class, my father had become a part of history by serving in the Office of Strategic Services (OSS) during World War II. He had been sworn to secrecy for twenty-five years after the war.

When I was born, Dad was the pastor of a church. As I grew up listening to his sermons, I learned about the Bible, Dad's experiences growing up on his family's farm, and eventually, OSS stories. During every Christmas season, Dad exchanged Christmas cards with a few of his OSS friends. I loved reading the cards and seeing pictures he received from them. The cards represented a mysterious life my dad had lived before my existence.

Through the years after the war, Dad occasionally met with OSS friends and their families. Then in 2000, my husband and daughter and I were visiting Pastor Gerald Nilsen and his wife in Moorhead, Minnesota, which is next door to Fargo, North Dakota. Hans Halverson, one of my dad's OSS cohorts, lived in Fargo. Dad gave me Hans's telephone number, and I called. I was a bit nervous because I hadn't met Hans. The phone rang a few times before I heard a message asking me to leave my name and number. I explained that I was Benny McCoy's daughter and that I was in Moorhead and would like to meet him and his wife. Hans and LaVerne returned my call soon and invited us to meet them at a restaurant. When we arrived at the restaurant, I recognized Hans from pictures he had sent Dad.

"I would recognize you anywhere," Hans said. "You look just like Benny."

I learned that the Nilsens, like Hans Halverson, had family in Norway. Through Pastor Nilsen, connections were made with Arne Nilsen, who you will learn about in a later chapter.

Hans was the first of my dad's OSS friends that I met. In 2001, Dad and I arranged a group meeting in Brownsville, Texas, with Hans and his wife and two more OSS friends, Francis Knapp and Lloyd Postel. This was the second gathering of this OSS group in Brownsville. Al Clark, now deceased, had convened with the group at the first Brownsville reunion. Dad; my brother, Darrell; and I flew to Brownsville, Texas, for the meeting at Tipotex Chevrolet. I think all of the men would agree with me that recalling their OSS experiences would have been easier for them twenty years prior to that meeting. Each one remembered incidents that the others had forgotten. It was comical to listen to their different versions of the tales they all remembered.

This book primarily consists of their memories of the years previous to, during, and since World War II. Additional stories have been included that describe the experiences of others who were either a part of the OSS or the European theater of World War II. The stories reflect each individual's perspective, and thus, they provide a uniquely personal vantage point from which to examine World War II.

People from various walks of life were chosen to serve in the OSS Dad, Hans, Francis, Lloyd, Don, and Al worked specifically in OSS Communications. While they were from different parts of the country and family backgrounds, I noticed an interesting phenomenon in my research for this book: all of these men have been married just once. Family members told Dad and his friends after the war that when they were investigated, questions were asked about their family, school, and the types of friends they hung around with, along with other details. Apparently, family values were important for the type of job these particular men were responsible for in communications. I further observed this phenomenon in leaders of World War II and other OSS members. Having seen how important these values are to these men, I integrated a look into their family backgrounds into this book.

So I pass this baton to you. Take it, and pass it to others so that it can continue throughout generations as their treasure of recorded memories.

PART 1
THE HOME FRONT

INTRODUCTION

ANGELA HORN

ֆ❀

FAMILY BACKGROUND INFLUENCES each individual for a lifetime. A person's background doesn't change. However, habits can be learned or unlearned. It doesn't matter if you came from a rich, poor, good, or bad background; what matters is what you make of it. My paternal grandmother, Arzelia, taught my dad a lesson that was handed down to me: "You can do anything you set your mind to."

The following people were faced with a situation beyond their control—war. They came from various types of backgrounds, yet they came together in the war effort for one purpose—freedom.

Benny McCoy: Benard and Arzelia McCoy, my grandparents, named my dad "Benard Horace" and called him by his middle name. Later he changed the spelling of his middle name to "Harace" because he didn't want anyone to pronounce his name as "Horse." It wasn't until he was in the Army that he was nicknamed "Benny."

Dad's parents were sharecroppers in East Texas, about two miles from the Angelina River. Their first baby had died with lung congestion, or pneumonia, thirteen months prior to Dad's birth. But Dad was born a healthy weight—thirteen pounds and six ounces!

The principle means of livelihood in East Texas during the early 1900s were ranching, farming, and railroad construction. Grandpa Benard worked as a "tie hacker"—he contracted with the railroad to furnish ties, or timbers, to place in the roadbed for iron rails that trains could travel on.

Francis Knapp: South Texas was home for Francis. His dad was an automobile and farming entrepreneur. From him, Francis learned entrepreneurial skills that would benefit him later in life.

Hans Halverson: Hans was born into the Scandinavian community of Northwood, North Dakota. Hans spoke Norwegian prior to English. His maternal grandmother lived next door to the family and insisted on speaking only Norwegian when conversing with him. He used the language widely throughout his early years and in school. Hans inherited his father's

1

entrepreneurial abilities and began his own business investments at an early age.

Lloyd Postel: Lloyd grew up in California, in a family mostly of German descent. His maternal and paternal grandparents had moved to the United States from Europe, settled in San Francisco, and opened businesses there.

Don Brunette: Don's background was Italian. His father was born in a little town called Torre Santa Suzanna in southern Italy, but he lived most of the time in Rome before coming to the United States. Don's mother was born in Taranto, Italy, and came to the United States around 1910. His parents met and married in New York and had five children. Three of their children served in World War II. Don's two brothers were already in service in the armored division when Don, the youngest, received his call.

Al Clark: Al Clark grew up in Detroit, Michigan. Al's father, once a successful businessman, lost all that he had in the Depression. Al told Dad that because his parents couldn't afford the complete tuition, he washed dishes so that he could get a pharmaceutical degree. He was successful and became a pharmacist before he was drafted. (Sadly, he passed away before I began writing this book, so I could not record his personal memories. But the others include him within their recollections.)

Arne Nilsen: Arne Nilsen, the last child of eight, grew up on a farm near Larvik, Norway. His father, a seaman for several years, was Chief Mate on board different tall ships (sailing ships). My friend Pastor Gerald Nilsen, whose dad was Arne's first cousin, said Arne's dad left the sea for good in 1917 and then worked at the Treshcow Fritzoe Paper Mill in Larvik until he retired.

It was at Poundon, a community near London, England, that Dad met Francis, Hans, Lloyd, Don, and Al. When they arrived in Poundon, they knew little about how and why they had been selected for the OSS However, the OSS was learning about them on the home front by interrogating their families, friends, schools, and employers.

On the home front, my mother and mother-in-law worked to support the war effort. My mother, Myrl, worked at a mill in her community. As men left for the war, the women took up the slack to fill the mill's vacancies. Mother made flagpoles of all sizes for ships until the mill was shut down after a fire. After the mill closed, she worked at a sewing factory and also a restaurant in a college town. Fern, my mother-in-law, did her part at an airplane plant when men went off to war.

2

Often today, marriages are made to keep "as long as you get along," but in the World War II era, marriages were made to keep "'til death do you part." In studying the lives of WWII leaders, I particularly noticed choices they made that exemplified morals from their upbringing, standards they kept in spite of any desire that any of them may have had to do otherwise. In their leadership, family values were their guide as they made decisions, both personal and political, that would affect their families and country.

In leadership, one must be willing to be on display—to live in a glass house. I can relate because I grew up in a pastor's home. I recall a discussion once about the family of a minister. When the preacher walks up to the pulpit to minister to the people, he steps into another role—alone. The family sits in the audience with the parishioners, the saints.

The wife of a minister, or leader, also experiences the lonely road. Her husband may be praised; he may be criticized. A wise lady will smile and press on. My mother would always smile at church. She might have had an awful day, but one wouldn't see a frown on her face.

To minister is to sacrifice, to smile in spite of the pain, to choose the lonely road. But the rewards can be great. So it is with the ministers of our country, those who lead us in confidence, in peace, and in war. Like Dad, Francis, and many in the OSS group, some World War II leaders grew up on farms. One had German-speaking parents like Lloyd. One factor was the same for all, however. All grew up families with strong morals. A look at the values that were important during World War II and to OSS leaders and this OSS group shows that family values have changed since the WWII era.

FRANKLIN DELANO ROOSEVELT

Raised least like this OSS group, Franklin Delano Roosevelt, who was born to aristocratic parents in the late 1800s, was accustomed to wealth. Roosevelt held one thing in common with this OSS group—a strong moral upbringing in an era when marriage was highly regarded and divorce was frowned upon. Any thought of divorce between Franklin and Eleanor was overruled by Franklin's mother, Sara Roosevelt. Apparently, Franklin didn't feel that he was too old to listen to his mother, even though he was married with a family. Franklin and Eleanor remained together, if not for love, certainly because of loyalty to their family. According to Bonnie Angelo in *First Mothers*, "Eleanor turned to her mother-in-law for help. In 1918, she made a shocking discovery: her husband was in love with her secretary, Lucy Mercer. After confronting her husband, Eleanor offered him a divorce. Sara did not take this development calmly. Eleanor might have been willing to give up without a fight, but Sara would not. By all accounts, there was a tense discussion with her son, in which she made it clear that the scandal of divorce would foreclose any thought of a political career and would poison his entire life.[1]

Dwight D. Eisenhower

Dwight David Eisenhower, also born in the late 1800s, grew up on a farm in a family that knew hard times and required their children to share farm and field daily chores in a home in which strict moral values were revered. Dad saw Dwight Eisenhower on numerous occasions, some of them were in Paris while marching at the head of contingent of soldiers on parade, especially on the Avenue des Champs-Élysées. Dad remembers seeing Eisenhower getting in his car with his chauffeur, a lady whom Dad assumes was Kay Summersby—the woman Eisenhower allegedly had an affair with.

According to the book *Past Forgetting, My Love Affair With Dwight D. Eisenhower*, the man who would later be president stated, "If there are two paths a man can take, both of them honorable, then all things being equal, he should take the path along which he will do the most good, inflict the least hurt."[2] Could Eisenhower have made that statement thinking of Mamie and Kay Summersby? Whatever happened, Ike stayed married to Mamie. Obviously, loyalty to family overruled any desires outside of marriage vows in the Eisenhower home.

Harry S. Truman

The Truman family strikes me as one that especially considered loyalty to be of high importance. Harry S. Truman's parents honored both of their fathers by naming their son after them. The two fathers both had names that began with an "S," but they were different names; therefore, little Harry was given a middle initial, not a middle name. And Harry S. Truman accomplished a feat that few men would agree to—his mother-in-law lived with him and his wife.

It's helpful to look at the values that contributed to making great men and women who lead into the people they are. The memories of World War II, the OSS, and the home front that my parents, my dad's OSS comrades, my mother-in-law, and others have shared with me exemplify many of these values. They describe the way families lived, how the war effort was supported at home and abroad, and how America transitioned back to normal living after the war.

Part One presents Dad and his OSS friends as they heard about Pearl Harbor and leads up to their introduction to the OSS.

BENNY McCOY

ॐ

Benny McCoy before going to war

Benny McCoy

THAT LIFE-CHANGING DAY IN DECEMBER OF 1941

"HEY, MAC, HAVE you heard the news?" a customer asked me when he pulled up at the service station where I worked.

"No, I haven't," I said. "I've been busy. What is it?"

"The Japs just bombed Pearl Harbor."

"Did they do any damage?"

"They sank every ship the United States Navy had."

"That doesn't sound good."

"They bombed it with planes. It's a mess."

Monday morning at school, the announcement was made that we would be having school six days a week the rest of that term so that we could end school early to work in defense plants. That's what I remember about December 7, 1941.

When I was two years and two months old, my father was stricken with what the doctor called "galloping consumption." Mother buried my dad and was left penniless. Relatives helped with the burial expenses. The next year, she worked at various places to sustain herself and provide for me. She became acquainted with a good man who had lost his wife in death. He had six children living at home and two children who had already married. This friendship culminated in a marriage that would endure for forty-six years.

My stepfather, Tom Wall, "Papa," was an avid cow man and rancher. By the time I was ten years old, I could ride any horse or mule on the farm and handle any plow with mules pulling it. At eleven, I was milking the cows that provided milk for the family and could drive any vehicle. No driver's license was required in those days.

6

By the time I was fourteen, the youngest of my stepbrothers was married. That left my younger half-sister, Vera, and me as the only children at home. Mother arranged for me to move in with her parents, Grandpa Joe and Grandma Della Russell, in Huntington, Texas, to further my education. She took me eighteen miles to San Augustine, Texas, and dropped me off about a mile or two outside of San Augustine on the Nacogdoches highway. I was fifteen years old.

She asked me, "Have you ever hitchhiked?"

I said, "No, ma'am."

She said, "I think you stick your thumb up," and she held her hand out with her thumb pointing straight up to illustrate.

Mother left me there with my little pasteboard box with all my clothes in it. I held my thumb out, pointing up, and within ten minutes, a brand-new Buick rolled up.

The driver said, "Where are you going, son?"

I said, "I want to catch a ride to Nacogdoches. I'm on my way to Huntington to live with my grandma and grandpa."

He said, "I'm going to Nacogdoches. I can carry you that far." He told me he was the pastor of the Baptist church in San Augustine. Boy, I was glad he was a preacher. I felt good about it because you heard stories about San Augustine. It had a notorious reputation; they had gun battles and killed people.

I got in his car. It was thirty-five miles from San Augustine to Nacogdoches. The man dropped me off on the Lufkin side of Nacogdoches, where I caught another ride, this time with a man driving a pickup. He dropped me off at Redland, Texas. After a couple more rides, I made it to my grandparents' house in Huntington. That is where I graduated from high school and was living when I heard the news of Pearl Harbor.

For one year I attended a junior college. After that year, Stone and Webster Engineering Corporation hired me as a steam fitter clerk. In that capacity, I helped in constructing a synthetic rubber plant for making tires for the war effort. For about six months I worked and made $52 a week. That was pretty good for a seventeen-year-old kid. One of my responsibilities was to keep every blueprint up to par. The blueprints had to be brought up-to-date every day. I was required to write letters about the blueprints, and those letters were given to the chief engineer for his signature. The engineers treated me well and helped me to learn quickly. I gained a lot of satisfaction from working with them.

One day in the early part of 1943, I received a letter in the mail that interrupted my job at Stone and Webster. My "friends and neighbors" had selected me to answer the call to selective service in the Army of the United States of America. My life was put on hold for me to go to war.

College and employment were temporarily suspended until after the war. Marriage, however, could not wait. I had fallen in love with Myrl Morehead from Huntington, Texas. Myrl and I were married June 7, 1943, just before I left for the Army.

Following the Army's instructions, I left for Tyler, Texas, to be inducted. At Tyler, everybody was given a physical and a number. We put our clothes in a place with that same number on it. We were also given a little bag with a loop on it to put on our wrists. Any valuables had to be held in our hands.

The guy ahead of me was given number thirteen. He threw it back at them and said, "You're not giving me number thirteen and sending me over there to be killed!"

They turned to me, and I said, "I'll take it. It's a good number." I often wondered what happened to the guy. The number thirteen didn't have a thing to do with coming home from the war. I took number thirteen and came home safely.

From Tyler, I went to a reception center at Camp Walters in Mineral Wells, Texas. At the reception center, I read this sign: "Take Typing Test Here." I said to the boy sitting beside me, "Let's take a typing test."

He asked, "Can you type?"

"Yeah, I can type," I answered.

He asked, "Well, what are you doing over here waiting for the infantry? Get over there, and take a typing test. If you don't go, I'll drag you."

I went to the sergeant, a tough and crusty guy, and said, "I'd like to take a typing test."

He asked in a gruff tone, "Can you type?"

I said, "Yes, sir, I can type."

He said, "If I give you a typing test and you wind up here with forty words a minute, you can forget it."

I said, "I can beat that." I think I typed sixty-seven, and I was scared half to death.

The gruff sergeant said, "Yes, you can type. I'll put that on your service record. It will make a difference what you do."

From Mineral Wells, Texas, to Fort Knox, Kentucky

From Mineral Wells, Texas, I took a Kansas City Southern Railroad train to Fort Knox, Kentucky. The trip took several hours and was several hundred miles. Meals were eaten in a restaurant car. Fifty to seventy-five troops were transferring to Fort Knox on the train. When it was time to eat, the sergeant in charge went to the restaurant car to pay for the soldiers' meals with a requisition. However, he found out that the requisition didn't have his name on it. Instead, my name, Private Benny McCoy, was listed on the requisition along with my Army serial number.

The sergeant initiated a search party of soldiers to find me, but the soldiers couldn't find me. Finally, the sergeant told the train official that the train would have to stop in order to send a wire to report me as "absent without leave" (AWOL).

A boy from Lufkin, Texas, who overheard the sergeant's request, said, "McCoy is not AWOL. He's on the train." He directed the sergeant to me.

The sergeant said, "I thought you were AWOL. I'm glad they found you because your name is on the meal tickets. You'll have to sign the tickets before we can eat." I felt flabbergasted by this news. It was quite an experience.

Fort Knox, Kentucky—Training for Battle

In battle training, you are crawling and machine guns are shooting bullets thirty-six inches above the ground. You had better keep your head down and not even try to stand up. Those machine guns are set, and they shoot straight. You are told before you jump off through the infiltration course that those are real bullets. "Don't stand up unless you want to execute yourself and sign your demise from this world." They tell you so many things to make you angry. There were also signs on trees: "Learn to hate! Learn to kill!" They may not do that anymore. Maybe they have a different way to teach you to kill.

I griped every day that I was in training, wishing that I were at home. I wanted out. There was another soldier who was also sick and tired of it. When he walked around the grounds, he picked up every piece of paper he saw. He would read it and say, "That's not it." They thought he had lost his mind. Eventually, they called him in and gave him a discharge. He looked at the discharge paper and said, "That's it!"

The angriest I ever became in the Army was during the last week of our battle training. We took an eighteen-mile hike with a thirty-pound pack on our backs. We ran five minutes and walked five minutes. We were given three ten-minute fall-outs during the hike. Once we reached bivouac, we were allowed thirty minutes to eat and set up our tents. Thirty minutes after we went to bed, the fall-out woke us up. It was raining. We headed back with our packs, clothes, and boots wet. The boots slid up and down on our heels. After a while, the hide wore off, and our heels were rubbed raw. We went back eighteen miles in the rain while running five minutes and then walking five minutes, with three ten-minute fall-outs, just like we had begun.

Soldiers were sent to Fort Knox to become more hardened as troops. Fort Knox was an armored school, and for eight weeks I received training in army administration and learned clerical skills. There I received training in military intelligence and was given a code name when I became an undercover spy. I was instructed to pay close attention to important equipment. If there were any suspicious characters suspected of damaging equipment or if I noticed any unusual activity against the war effort, I was instructed to report the information to my superior, who was a sergeant. Every week I was required to mail a report to the address the sergeant had given me. I was given an official pass for whenever I was not on duty to go to town to visit my wife. That Class A pass was quite an honor. After graduation, I was sent across the Atlantic to Europe.

From Boston, Massachusetts, to Europe

When I left to go overseas, it was wintertime in Boston. It had snowed, and about eighteen inches of snow covered the ground. It was snowing as I walked over the gangplank. I looked down at that cold water and prayed, "God, don't let me die in this war!"

My overseas journey began on the *USS Uruguay*. The generator went out after we had been out a day or two, and we were tugged back to Boston, Massachusetts. We stayed at Camp Miles Standish in Boston. When I left Boston the second time, I went on the *USS George Washington*. There were 10,000 troops on that transport. It took a week to cross the Atlantic. We were told that because the North Atlantic was so cold, you couldn't live more than ten minutes if you went overboard. Besides that, U-boats were out there looking for us.

There were four rows of bunks, and I slept on the top bunk. I was sitting on the bunk one day during a bad storm. The ship was rolling and pitching when we heard a loud noise. The ship listed thirty to forty-five degrees. Suddenly, about a foot of water rushed across the floor.

The "abandon ship" alarm sounded, and I didn't climb down—I jumped. I grabbed my life preserver and headed for the deck with everyone else. We stayed there about an hour. Finally, we were allowed to go back down.

Someone had left some portholes open. When the ship rolled, the ocean rushed in. If you think you might have only ten minutes to live, you'll do some praying.

On the *George Washington*, I got sick from sleeping right under the portholes. To keep the cold air from blowing on me, I would jam a pillow in the porthole above me. When I fell asleep, another soldier would pull the pillow out because he would feel hot. I would wake up freezing.

Our ship landed in Liverpool, England, and we disembarked in the wee hours of March 11, 1944—my nineteenth birthday. We rode a train to Bath, England, about two hours west of London. When the train stopped, I was still sick. We were taken to our billets (what the British called "tents"). There were six men to a tent. For exercise endurance training, we were required to run a certain distance. Until we reached the necessary distance, we would run five minutes and walk five minutes. During this training, I began to cough incessantly. A fellow soldier, Reynolds, said, "McCoy, if you can stop this running every five minutes, you can get over that cough." He continued, "When they take their first break, let's slip off, and we'll hide out all day and cover up with leaves. I'll stay with you. You'll get over this cough." At the break we went off in the woods and hid all day long.

That afternoon when our group came back by, running five minutes and walking five minutes, Reynolds recognized them and said, "Let's go."

A guy who walked through found us and jumped on our case and told us to fall into a different group. I said, "Boy, we're in a mess now."

Reynolds said, "When they go over that little hill, let's run back to our group." We ran back to our group, and my coughing finally stopped. Reynolds was a brave guy.

I was transferred to a replacement depot in Bath and worked in the orderly room, the office where soldiers picked up supplies. While I was there, I was required to act as the supply sergeant and to type requisitions for troops' supplies. It was so cold in that office that a soldier held a heater turned towards my hands as I typed.

For battle, a soldier had fifty to sixty pounds of supplies packed on his back—supplies such as a gun, gas mask, clothing, and other things he'd need in country. Brooks Brothers made the uniforms, and Abercrombie and Fitch provided the supplies.

While in Bath I was directed to the captain's office. He was in charge of placement of soldiers. He said, "Don't come back here tomorrow. You're going to London."

"What am I going to London for?" I asked.

11

He replied, "I don't know. You have to report to the OSS, and I don't know what that is or what you'll be doing. I assume that it is the Office of Service and Supply."

The next day, I went to London. I was ushered into the enlisted men's barracks. Later, I was summoned by a captain for an interview. I followed him into his office. There was a chair on each side of his desk. He said, "Have a seat. I have a question for you. Are you willing to go beyond the call of duty?"

I said, "If it is necessary for my country, I can offer myself to save my country. I wouldn't do it to be a hero."

He said: "I think that's the answer we want."

After that, I was transported to Poundon Hill and assigned duty in the OSS.

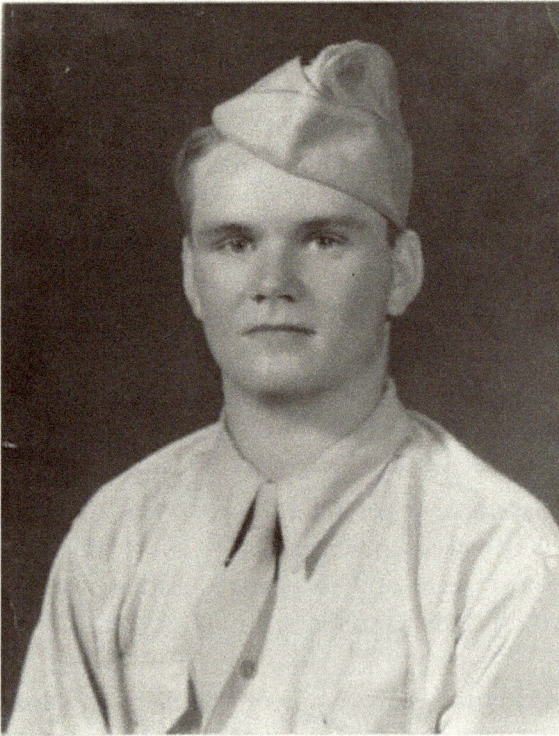

Benny McCoy

Benny McCoy with his mother's sister, Abbie Vetetoe, and aunt's friend

Benny McCoy (far right) with his mother, Arzelia Russell McCoy Wall; his sister, Vera Wall; his stepfather, Tom Wall; and his stepbrother Desmond Wall

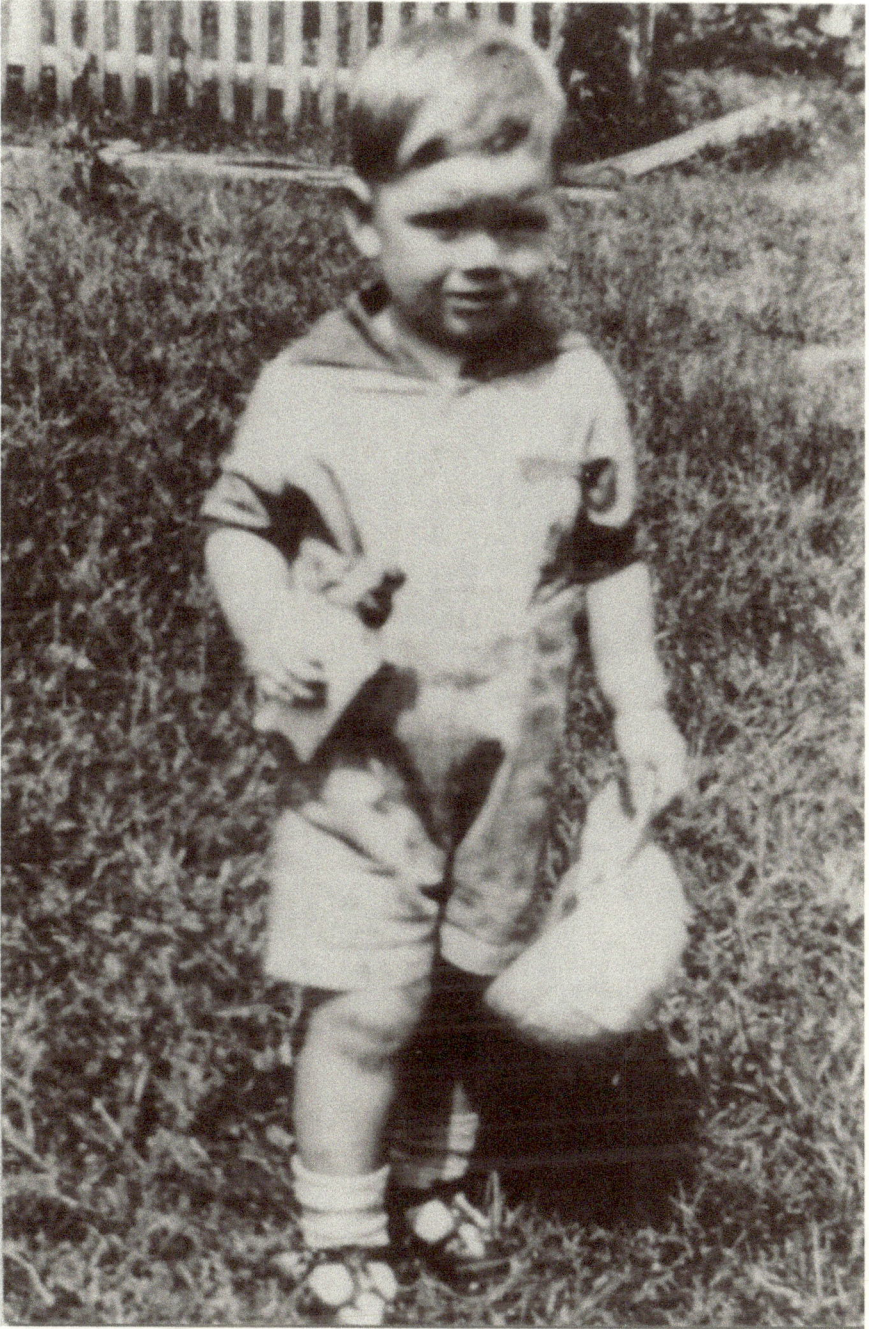

Benny McCoy

Benard Daniel McCoy, Benny McCoy's father

Vacant Lot where Brown's Service Station was
(where Benny was working when he heard about Pearl Harbor)

Church Parsonage (side door) in Huntington, TX, where
Benny and Myrl McCoy were married

17

Chapter 2

FRANCIS KNAPP

ಬಾ

MY FATHER MOVED to South Texas after beginning business with Ford Motor Company. His Model T history goes back to World War I. He had attended Officer Candidate School (OCS) and had just become an officer when the war ended. When he moved to South Texas, he called on the dealers. Initially, he assembled Model Ts. Eventually, he started his own Model T dealership in Donna, Texas. In 1921, he built a building that housed his operations for a long time. He moved to Weslaco, Texas, Francis Knapp's OSS ID and changed to the Chevrolet business after a dispute with Ford. He built dealerships in various Texas cities: Houston (1939), Brownsville (1935), Harlingen (1934), and Mercedes (early 1930s).

In the midst of building automobile dealerships, my dad, who liked farming, bought farmland and ended up in the citrus business. He became one of the three largest citrus growers in the Rio Grande Valley. At one time, he owned 1,100 acres of citrus. He also planted cotton, so he needed a gin. The gin served more than one purpose. We needed the gin for the grapefruit and other citrus when we couldn't pack it out.

My family also operated a canning business. The Knapp-Sherrill Canning Company in Donna, Texas began, about 1938. Originally, they farmed citrus and operated a juice plant. They developed several brands, like Texas Magic. The company produced orange and grapefruit juice. Later, however, the company grew carrots, tomatoes, chilies, black-eyed peas, sauerkraut, green beans, and anything else that made a little money. The family-owned Ro*Tel company, of which I was the chairman of the board, was sold fourteen years ago.

Until I graduated and went to college, I helped with the farming. The war interrupted my college plans, and I was inducted into the Army. After I was inducted at Fort Sam Houston in San Antonio, I went to Fort Hood in Killeen, Texas, for basic training, 141st Battalion. I thought I wanted to be in the Air Force. I knew I couldn't fly, but I wanted to do something mechanical, and I figured that the Air Force was the next best thing. It looked like I was going to be in a tank destroyer as a gunner in mechanics.

Luckily, there was another Aggie from Texas A & M University in the Air Force with me. I told him, "It looks like they don't have me placed right." Instead of the Air Force, I ended up at Fort Hood in clerk school, typing—the thing that may have saved my life. After Fort Hood, I went to Fort George G. Meade in Baltimore, Maryland, for further training.

I shipped out toward Liverpool on the *USS Uruguay*. The generator went out on the ship, and we came back to Camp Miles Standish in Boston. When the ship was repaired, we took it to Liverpool. Everybody on board took sick. I remember being on the bottom bunk. Why I was on the bunk, I couldn't figure out. I thought I was supposed to be up doing something, but it wasn't long until I realized why; I got up right quick—sick. We were a sick bunch.

Finally, we reached the harbor at Liverpool. From Liverpool, I went to Wales for a while and then to London for a week or two. After London, I went to Poundon to work for the OSS. Individuals in the OSS were constantly monitored. They received a special identity card called a "Class A Pass," which I have kept. The Class A Pass gave the OSS personnel liberty to visit anywhere in a foreign country in which a member of the OSS was working.

I still meet with the bunch from Fort Hood that I was with in the OSS. I think we're just about through meeting, though, because we had a group that was pretty old to begin with, and some of us aren't able to meet anymore. The older ones of the group were thirty-two years old when we were drafted, and we younger ones were eighteen years old. Every one of us ended up with an excellent clerical job in the war.

Francis Knapp and Benny McCoy

Chapter 3

HANS HALVERSON

ℰℭ

Hans Halvorson and Benny McCoy

WHILE I WAS working one summer at a hardware store, I noticed a plentiful supply of small bamboo canes. A community celebration was coming up soon. I asked the owner what I could buy the canes for. He said, "A nickel apiece."

I said to my friend, "For the celebration, I'll ask my dad if we can take the big scale out of the bank lobby. We'll put it out on the corner and guess people's weights. If we guess their weight within three pounds, they give us a dime. If we miss by more than three pounds, we give them a cane—and still have a nickel profit."

President Roosevelt had just declared a national bank holiday, which meant all of the country's banks had to close for four days. If the banks didn't have the money to stay open, they couldn't reopen after the holiday. The day before the holiday, a farmer came into the bank where my father worked and told my father he wanted to take his savings out.

"OK, you can take it out," my father said. "That's your money, but will you be here at 3:00, when the bank closes today? Tomorrow is the bank holiday, and this will be the last day this bank will be open if you take your money out today. I want to give you the key and let you be the last one to lock the door."

The farmer left his money in the bank, and the bank reopened after the holiday.

The evening President Franklin Roosevelt reached into the lottery drum to pull out the initial World War II draft numbers, my name was the first one called out for my part for the country. I was number one, so there was no doubt about my going to war. I was staying at the YMCA and was sick the day my name was drawn, but my mother heard the announcement and fainted.

I visited Senator Langer about not going overseas. He sat at a large desk, and I sat across from him. He didn't smoke cigars—he chewed them with the cellophane still on them. He'd chew half of the cigar, and then he'd turn it around and chew the other half. Then he'd throw it in the waste paper basket. I suppose I sat there a half an hour, and he went through three or four cigars.

Because I was Scandinavian and knew how to speak Norwegian, I was sent to the University of Wisconsin for a year to take a refresher course in that language and to learn German. Next, I was supposed to learn how to jump out of an airplane because the Germans had taken over Norway. The United States was going to drop into Norway. But before I finished, it was all over with. The Germans had been kicked out of Norway. Since there was no more need for me in Norway, I was sent to England and ended up typing in the OSS. I had not heard of the OSS before I went to England.

Chapter 4
LLOYD POSTEL

ℰℭ

Lloyd Postel on left

THOUGH MY FAMILY wasn't rich, we lived in a wealthy enclave, a bedroom community north of San Francisco. My dad commuted across San Francisco Bay on the ferries and on the train until they built a bridge.

The last couple of years before World War II, he commuted on the bus.

Both of my parents were born in San Francisco, and all of my grandparents were born in Europe. One grandparent was French, but the others were German. My mother spoke German at home and did not learn English until she went to school when she was five or six years old. My father could not speak German at all, and from that I inferred that they didn't speak that much of it in his household (my grandparents' home); although, my grandfather was a very German type. I knew him very briefly when I was a kid.

Both sets of grandparents owned saloons in San Francisco. One of them was located at Front and Pine, which is right downtown. In 1906, it was wiped out with an earthquake and fire. At that time, my grandparents took my mother, who was still a kid, to Germany to see the relatives. It took a week to reach the boat and another week to travel to Europe once they were on the boat and then the same coming home. It was really a big deal then.

One of the relatives told my grandmother, "You shouldn't have spent all this money. You should have just sent the money and stayed at home"—and meant it, I guess.

On December 7, 1941, I was playing in a football game near Mill Valley, California. Some guy was running up the road saying, "The Japanese bombed Pearl Harbor."

We said, "Yeah, and you've got the Golden Gate Bridge for sale."

He convinced us. We went to listen to the radio, and sure enough, we heard the news—it was a shock.

My father felt that there was no such thing as a Greek American or a German American or any other kind of American. He was strong-minded about this. The fact that I was of German descent never crossed my mind until the OSS recruited me in Washington.

At nineteen, I enlisted in Marin County, California, and was inducted in San Francisco six months later. Next, I was sent to the Presidio of Monterey, a reception center. I was there about five days. After that, I went to basic training at a camp called Kohler. There I learned how to march and shoot a rifle.

They gave us a lot of tests. One night my name showed up on a bulletin board. My name was one of fourteen listed. When I saw my name on the board, I knew I would be leaving Kohler. From Kohler I went to Salt Lake City, another reception area. At the University of Utah, I lived in the field house.

After Salt Lake City, I was sent to Madison, Wisconsin, for basic training and language school to learn Italian. At Madison, I was introduced to the OSS. A redheaded second lieutenant from Washington, D.C., administered five paragraphs of gibberish to us as a test. He handed it out and refused to tell us what to do with it. I discovered that if you used every fourth letter out of the paragraph, you got a message out of it. I guess I passed it, because I wound up in the OSS.

After about ten months at Madison, I went to a Girl Scout Camp in northern Virginia—this was kind of a holding area. By the time we arrived in Virginia, we had the idea that we were involved in an information system.

About a month after leaving Madison, I arrived in Europe. The trip lasted about a week and a half. The *Aquitania* docked in Glasgow, Scotland, with about 13,000 soldiers on board. I took a train to London. After a couple of days there, I rode a train to Poundon.

After Lloyd arrived in Madison, Wisconsin, at language school, he met Don Brunette. He met Benny, Francis, Hans, and Al at Poundon, near London.

Arne Nilsen is introduced later, in the European Theater section of *Phantom Seven*. He was not a member of the OSS.

Chapter 5

DON BRUNETTE

ℒ

Photo of Don Brunette

I WAS ATTENDING The College of New York when the call came. I was inducted into the Air Force in January of 1943 and completed my basic training in Atlantic City, New Jersey. Just before my outfit was scheduled to go to Camp Crowder in Missouri, I was asked if I would be willing to volunteer for the OSS. I had a language background in Italian and had studied French for three years. I was told I would go to the University of Wisconsin to increase my proficiency in those languages. I said, "yes," and away I went.

When I arrived in Wisconsin, I was placed in a German program, studying German most of the day. My background of Italian and French went out the window. I completed my program, and as I recall, I was sent to Washington, D.C., before going to England.

I remember meeting Lloyd Postel there. He was from Wisconsin. He was in the Italian program. We sailed together to England on the *Aquitania*, a troop ship. It was a fast boat, and we didn't have a convoy. Lloyd was not a very good sailor and got sick quickly and often. There were German subs in the North Atlantic, and the *Aquitania* had to zigzag frequently, which didn't help Lloyd's stomach condition.

When we first arrived in London (before Poundon), we stayed at Cadogan Square in the heart of London. That was during the time when German "buzz bombs" were flying overhead. No one ran until the bomb began to fall. Then you ran like sixty in the opposite direction!

Eventually, we left Cadogan and went to Poundon. I did not go to any clerk school and found myself in cryptography. My year of studying German and my knowledge of Italian and French went out the window.

Don Brunette and Benny McCoy

Don Brunette and Benny McCoy

Chapter 6

MEMORIES OF A COMRADE, AL CLARK

ANGELA HORN

∾

Francis Knapp, Benny McCoy, Al Clark, and Hans Halverson in Brownsville, Texas

AL CLARK HAD to put his life as a pharmacist on hold when he was drafted. Sent to England and later to France, he worked with Dad and the others of this OSS group in Poundon and in Paris with Dad, Francis, and Hans. Al was not a speedy typist, but he didn't make mistakes. He often worked on the shift with Dad, and Dad became Al's best friend.

Al talked to Dad about being from a poor family but wanting to marry the "Blueblood" girl from Michigan that he was in love with. Out of this OSS group, Al was the oldest, and Dad was the youngest. Dad, the only married one out of the group, married the girl he fell in love with before he went off to war. He was supportive of Al's desire to marry the Blueblood girl and assured him that being poor didn't matter if he loved her.

Chapter 7

HOME FRONT MEMORIES

ℰℭ

Benny McCoy's photo in a locket sent to his wife, Myrl

ANGELA HORN

WHILE DAD WAS at war, my mother, Archie Myrl, became involved with the war efforts in her community. She especially liked working with her Uncle Jack Due's wife, Dan. Whether or not Dan was a nickname, I don't know. My uncle Boots Morehead (he does have another name, Travis, though he's always been called Boots), said, "Uncle Jack and Aunt Dan is all we ever knew. I didn't know anything about a nickname." Mother and her nine siblings grew up in an East Texas community called Huntington. Maybe it was an East Texas trend to name girls after their fathers in the early 1900s. Mother was named after her father, Archie.

Myrl McCoy

Dan, my aunt, organized the county's bond sales and the community rallies that people attended to raise war bonds. Cakes and pies and box suppers were sold, and sometimes a queen was chosen—once my best friend was elected. The box suppers, which were usually held on the front lawn of my community's school, were auctioned off to the highest bidder. At these suppers, bonds were sold to honor a soldier. The box supper provided a dinner for two. The auctioneer announced the name of the cook and decorator of each box. Then the person who sold the most suppers won a prize.

At a box supper Harace and I attended just after we met, the auctioneer, who was drunk, bought many of the boxes himself. He would pick up a box and say, "I would pay $5 or $10 for that one myself." That started the bid. However, that night he started the bids so high that very few others could buy a box. He was the county commissioner and had money. The soldiers attending the box supper didn't have money and were outbid by the drunken auctioneer. That night, the box suppers were sold before Harace had the chance to buy the one I had brought.

Other community activities involved sending mail and giving going-away parties to the soldiers. We kept a list of soldiers from the county. Dan organized, and I assisted her. She would tell me about a soldier who hadn't received mail or goody packages. I would ask people who didn't have a relative serving in the war to write the soldier and send him a package of goodies. These packages were like cookies, cake, and chocolate often called "cheer mail."

At the going-away parties, hostesses would serve popcorn balls, parched peanuts, homemade cookies, and candy. There was also taffy pulling. We played games such as cakewalks, "four-hand-round," or "first-two-gents-across-the-hall." We considered these last two to be games, though others called them square dancing. The parties were held in large homes that had plenty of parking space outside, because nearly everyone in the community attended.

East Texas women often baked syrup teacakes. If they were low on sugar, they compensated with honey. For recipes requiring butter, it helped to own a cow. I helped my mother churn the butter. In our household, the cow supplied the dairy products.

A family I knew had a teenage boy who came home hungry one night. He saw a plate of biscuits on the table. He opened the fridge and found a pound of what looked like butter. He melted the butter over the plate of biscuits, poured syrup over the buttered biscuits, and feasted.

When he mentioned the buttered biscuits to his mother the next day, she said, "What do you mean, butter? I didn't have any butter in the refrigerator."

He said, "Oh, yes, you did. It was that new butter called margarine that you bought."

"That wasn't butter. That was lard that you ate," she told him.

My favorite piece of furniture in our home was a Lane cedar chest. When we were not busy working or helping in war efforts, my friends and I would encourage one another to make beautiful things for our homes that we would store in our cedar chests. We would share patterns to trace on linen tea towels, dresser scarves, pillowcases, and tablecloths. I have always treasured these embroidered pieces, displayed them in a special room, and shared the memories of them with family and friends.

Many rainy and cold nights we would pull our sewing baskets out and talk of our husbands and fiancés and the dream homes we would share with them after the war. This would keep girls from becoming too lonely while their loved ones were away for such long times.

My friend Dorothy and I worked in Nacogdoches, Texas, and roomed together. Occasionally, my grandmother brought us quilt patterns and taught us how to piece together quilt blocks with scraps we had saved. I saved scraps from all of the dresses I made. We would sit up late on Saturday nights and work on quilts. Sometimes we would go home on the weekends to visit, and Dorothy's mother would teach us how to quilt the blocks we had pieced together. Dorothy's mother lived about two miles from my mother.

I remember wearing rayon hose before fashionable nylons became popular. If worn when traveling, the rayon would cause the hose to stretch to the size of the knee and bulge out when you stood up. One time a friend asked me, "Myrl, what happened to your knee?" I was wearing rayon hose, and the knee area of the hose was bulging out.

After the war, Harace and I passed by a store in Washington D.C. that had a long line of people standing outside of it.

"Why the line?" Harace asked me.

"Oh, haven't you heard? They have nylon hose in," I told him. As a treat to me, he stood in the long line and bought me a pair of the nylons.

Women wore hats. Sweetheart necklaces and bracelets made with a little gold heart were popular. Harace surprised me with a sweetheart necklace on my birthday. A picture of him was placed on the inside. He had taken a picture only a few weeks after he entered the Army at Ft. Knox. I wore it at all times with his picture inside it. It was the first picture he had sent me. Sometimes at work, other women would ask me to look at their lockets and pictures, which always started a conversation about our sweethearts.

When I came home from work, I stopped by the post office. Harace wrote me every day. I would receive up to three of his letters every day. At a restaurant I liked, I would stop in and read my letters. Each night, I would write another. One time, for thirty days, I didn't hear from him. This happened about the time of the Battle of the Bulge. He said after that battle he received a stack of my letters all at once.

Sometimes I would go somewhere and the friend I roomed with or my sister would sneak my letters and read them. Later I discovered their secret. In order to keep them from reading my letters, I would have to burn some of them—which I regret.

BENNY McCOY

It was difficult for farmers to maintain their farms when their laborers went to war. When my stepdad lost his laborers to war, he bought a tractor to farm with. After the laborers returned from the war, he continued to use the tractor. He could plow more easily and accomplish more work.
The tractor plowed two rows at a time.

Victory gardens were planted to aid the home front with food. Anyone with suitable land for growing vegetables was encouraged to support the home front with canned goods.

Food was rationed into different categories, such as A, B, C, D, and K. Other rations were called "spares." These were for items that might be added to the list of rations.

Walking was very prominent during the war. Nobody thought a second time about walking a mile or two or more. Few vehicles were used for just one person. People shared rides and transportation. The federal government set the highway speed, nationwide, at thirty-five miles per hour. It took forever to get anywhere on the nation's highways. Trains were the best method of travel.

FRANCIS KNAPP

My dad stopped selling cars at his dealership. They didn't have the cars to sell. The automobile industry came to a halt in 1942.

FERN HORN

I worked on the final assembly of airplane engines in a war plant. There was a particular bolt that was difficult for me to tighten, and the inspector would always check it when he came by.

I released a man named George so he could go to war. "Thanks a lot. As soon as I get you broken in, I have to go to war," George said.

I used to write to some of the soldiers that I knew. Sometimes I wouldn't hear from them anymore, so I would assume they were no longer with us.

Our part of the war started on December 7, 1941, and I graduated from high school in 1941 at 17. Though I didn't smoke, I married a cigarette salesman. I remember a slogan from the Lucky Strike cigarettes: "LUCKY STRIKE GREEN HAS GONE TO WAR!" The Lucky Strike package was green with a white target. The green was taken off, and the packages were then made white with the little target on them. The dye used to make the packages green was needed for metal production. (According to Snopes, http://www.snopes.com/business/market/luckystrike.asp, "the bull's eye on the package was always red, and the decision to redesign the product's look was simply a business choice and would have been made war or no war.") There was a lot of good music during the war. I remember "Rosie, the Riveter" as a popular song. One of my favorite songs by Glenn Miller was "String of Pearls." His music sounded beautiful and was good dancing music. Another popular group, the Andrews Sisters, sang "Don't Sit Under the Apple Tree."

You could go to movies back in those days and enjoy them. Shirley Temple's bad treatment in the orphanage was the extent of violence then. And sex was only hinted at. As the sun set in the west, you could figure out what was happening but didn't see it. Now it's a spectator sport.

Certain foods, like sugar and meat, were rationed, but I don't remember going without. Clothes were rationed, and gasoline was rationed. We didn't go a lot of places. I lived in Wichita, Kansas, at the time, and the bus system was very good. If I had to go to town, I would ride the bus.

Myrl McCoy's locket from Benny

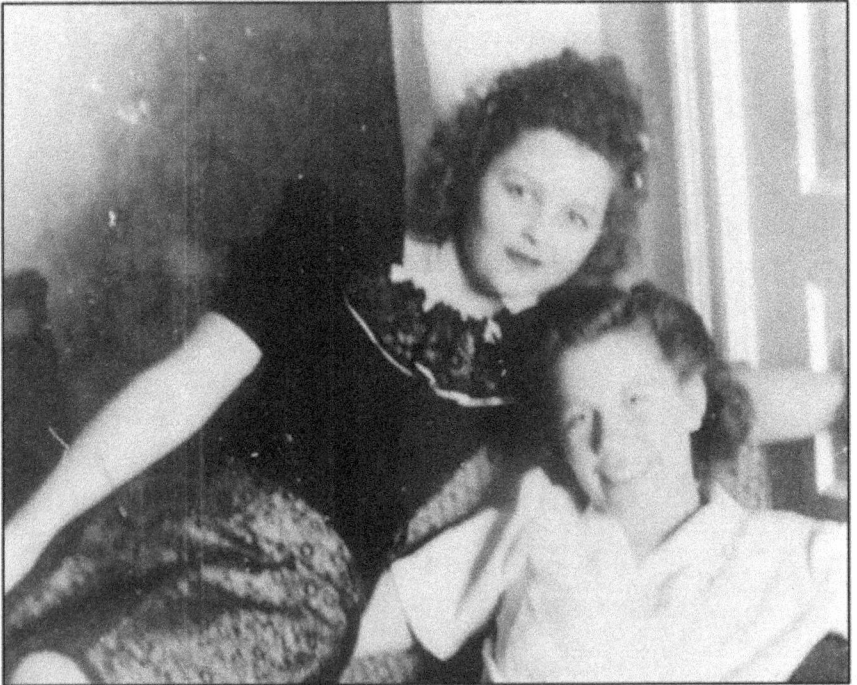

Myrl McCoy and best friend, Dorothy "Dot"

Myrl McCoy's pillowcases, quilts, and needlework, some of which she made
with her best friend, Dot, during WWII

Myrl McCoy and sister Phynice Morehead Fuller

Myrl McCoy and brother Henry Morehead

Myrl McCoy

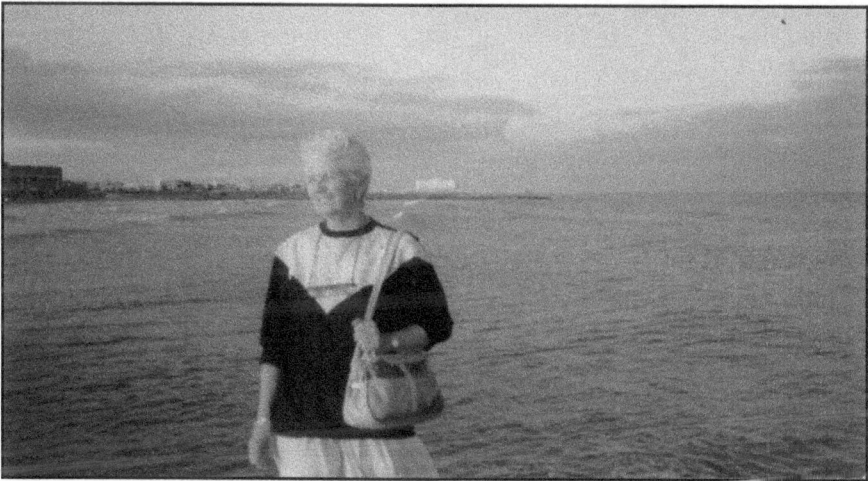

Fern Horn, Angela McCoy Horn's mother-in-law

Beatrice Morehead, Myrl McCoy's mother

Archie Morehead, Myrl McCoy's father

PART 2
EUROPEAN THEATER

INTRODUCTION

ℰꙄ

You ask, what is our policy? I will say: it is to wage war, by sea, land and air, with all our might and with all the strength God can give us: to wage war against a monstrous tyranny, never surpassed in the dark, lamentable catalogue of human crime. That is our policy. You ask, What is our aim? I can answer in one word: victory—victory at all costs, victory in spite of all terror, victory, however long and hard the road may be; for without victory, there is no survival.[3]

—Winston Spencer Churchill

Angela Horn

WHEN I MET Hans and LaVerne Halverson in Fargo, North Dakota, my husband was speaking at a church in Fargo's sister city, Moorhead, Minnesota. Pastor Gerald Nilsen learned of Dad's and Hans's OSS involvement during World War II. He told me about his cousin in Norway who was involved in the resistance of Norway during World War II. Through Pastor Nilsen, I contacted his cousin, Arne Nilsen of Norway. Arne shared his story with me and was gracious enough to allow me to include it in this book. Arne's and the other Norwegians' efforts for Norway's freedom during World War II were an integral factor that resulted in Hans working with my dad in the OSS.

Norway resisted Hitler's Nazis vigorously. The Norwegians assisted the agents in the resistance with blowing up the heavy-water plant that
Hitler had built for the production of uranium to make atom bombs. The Norwegians' efforts of resistance, such as the one Arne Nilsen participated in, were so effective that Hans Halverson was spared from being dropped into Norway. Instead, he decoded and encoded top-secret messages.

At our group meeting in Brownsville, Texas, Dad, Francis Knapp, Lloyd Postel, and Hans Halverson reminded one another of their experiences in England, France, and Italy.

Overlord

Phantom Seven's OSS men were ushered into the World War II European Theater of Operations (ETO) immediately after training. Their training and qualifications proved to be useful in Operation Overlord, the code name given to the Allied invasion of France scheduled for June 1944, specifically by

49

decoding and encoding top-secret messages communicated between the strategic leaders of the ETO and spies. They were all trained in London for the OSS and met at Poundon Hill, a place not far from London, where they began working for the OSS.

Dad well remembers that he was the one in his office who decoded and encoded the message to go ahead with Overlord on June 6. He also recalls that while he was at Poundon Hill, he sent messages to the spies about the preparations for Overlord and where to blow up the bridges. He said, "I sat and talked to spies that the OSS was preparing to drop in strategic locations."

After Operation Overlord and Eisenhower's announcement of Italy's unconditional surrender, Dad, Francis, Al, and Hans were sent to France, and Lloyd and Don were sent to Italy.

BENNY McCOY

There are several inescapable facts that helped the Allies win World War II over the Germans. There was Dwight Eisenhower, the military leader of all forces in Europe with and for the British. And then you had George S. Patton in his military leadership on the side of the English forces. Of course, we cannot downplay the commitment of the English military leaders, both in North Africa and in France.

The British were the people who suffered in North Africa. True, American military forces were used in North Africa, but Britain fought almost alone for a considerable time to keep North Africa from going to the Germans. Eisenhower served in North Africa by leading an army. Patton also served there. But the gathering of all the military forces hurled their military might against the Germans on June 6, 1944. It was this maneuver that brought about the complete overthrow of German power. Also, Russia had a part in bringing down Germany. They attacked Germany from the eastern side, and we attacked them from the western side.

France, of course, was the defeated nation. Through the might of England, America, and Russia assisting the French, their nation was saved. We would not want to forget to give credit to General DeGaulle and his leadership in restoring the French nation. He reorganized the political and military might of France and made it a free nation again. So looking at the situation as we see it today, there would not be a free Europe had the United States not intervened in the war.

I saw Churchill several times in different circumstances, like the marches on Champs-Élysées and in and around 10 Downing Street in London. Without Churchill, England possibly would have lost the war. Churchill paid a visit to the United States to ask Roosevelt for financial aid to furnish sea-going vessels to win the war in the English Channel over the Germans. Without America, England could not have defeated Germany. Who knows what the turn of events would have been between England and Germany if the United States had refused to enter the war. There is, of course, the fact of an atom bomb. It's just one man's opinion that Germany would have used the atom bomb if it would have helped them win the war.

When Churchill went before the House of Commons to get support for making the airplane, the Spitfire (the weapon and plane that would be used to defend England against the enemy), he said, "It will spit fire and destruction upon the enemy who will be trying to invade our shores." That was exactly what the plane was called, the Spitfire.

I remember Winston Churchill saying, "We shall overcome." That was his attitude toward Germany. He said if the Old World (England) could hold out until the New World (United States) came to Britain's assistance, they would prevail. He told Eisenhower he wanted to be in the invasion when we invaded France. Eisenhower told Churchill that he should not be in the invasion forces because it would not be safe for him, but Churchill insisted because he wanted to be where the action was. Eisenhower went to King George and told him that Churchill was insisting on being in the invasion forces. Eisenhower asked King George if he would help him change Churchill's mind. The king said he thought he could change his mind by telling him he would go too. When the king told Churchill he would go too, Churchill backed down.

Dad has always loved history and admired Churchill. He has often commented to me about Churchill's admirable qualities and has quoted some of the famous statements Churchill made. In addition to his leadership abilities, the charismatic Churchill was multi-talented as orator, author, craftsman, and painter. He was loved by Americans and was proclaimed an honorary citizen of the United States by President Kennedy. He was famous for his "never give in" philosophy and his often sharp-edged wit. For instance, one historian tells this story: "Lady Astor, a constant thorn in Churchill's side, once said in exasperation, 'Winston, if I were your wife, I'd put poison in your coffee.'

He replied without hesitation, 'Nancy, if I were your husband, I'd drink it.'"[4]

51

OFFICE OF STRATEGIC SERVICES

"William J. Donovan, the creator and director of the Office of Strategic Services (OSS), had performed distinguished military service in World War I. His insight on intelligence influenced President Roosevelt to appoint him chief of Coordinator of Information (COI) before Pearl Harbor. After Pearl Harbor, the COI changed to the OSS, and Donovan was made director. Thus, an intelligence organization had been created for the first time in the United States that brought together the work of intelligence collection and counterespionage, with the support of underground resistance activities, sabotage, and almost anything else in aid of our national effort that the regular armed forces were not equipped to do."[5]

The department of OSS Communications was vital in handling top-secret interaction among strategic World War II and OSS leaders, spies, and front lines. Lloyd Postel and my dad both remember meeting the leader of the OSS, William "Wild Bill" Donovan. Dad explains that there were two groups that the OSS employed: the civilians and the soldiers enlisted in the Army. Dad and his OSS friends were part of the United States Army group.

Donovan was another example of family loyalty and strict upbringing, and he was also married just once. His wife was from one of the wealthiest families in New York.

Dad describes Allen Dulles as "the most outstanding spy of the world that outranked William Donovan; although, Donovan was a protégé of F. D. Roosevelt." Dulles went to Switzerland, the spy center of World War II, and set up an office in Bern, the capital, known for its espionage and counterespionage interaction. In his book *The Secret Surrender*, Allen Dulles says, "My real tasks were to gather information about the Nazi and Fascist enemy and quietly to render such support and encouragement as I could to the resistance forces working against the Nazis and Fascists in the areas adjacent to Switzerland which were under the rule of Hitler or Mussolini."[6]

Chapter 8

RESISTANCE IN NORWAY

ହଡ

Arne Nilsen   Arne Nilsen and Family

HANS HALVERSON

JUST BEFORE THE Germans were driven out of Norway, the heavy-water plant was blown up. One of the men responsible for blowing up the plant came to Fargo, North Dakota. Often, friends and relatives of Fargo residents visit our city and receive an invitation to the Sons of Norway, an organization created by Fargo residents with Norwegian roots. The man who was connected to the heavy-water plant event visited my wife and me in our home. He had written a book about the heavy-water plant experience and shared the information with us. Since then, he passed away, and I have lost the information about his book.

ARNE E. NILSEN

It all began when I was about twelve or thirteen years old. My school teacher had been in Germany and had seen for himself how cruel Nazism

53

really was. He took me aside one day and told me all about it. Why me? Well, I was a good and clever pupil, I was interested in history and politics, and most of all, I looked and I was in my mind much older than my age. He told me: "A war will be coming, maybe this year, maybe one or two years from now [this was in 1937–38]. From what I have seen in Germany, this war will be the worst war we have ever had." He gave me a book called *Myrsoldater*, written by Wolfgang Langhoff. It was from a KZ (concentration) camp in Germany; you know, Hitler's government had such camps long before the war started.

Wolfgang Langhoff was a well-known writer, but he was a communist, and communists were sent to KZ camps as soon as Hitler took over. Langhoff had been in such a KZ camp himself, and he wrote about what it was like. At that time, it must have been in 1933–1935, they didn't even treat the prisoners very badly, not compared with what they did later on. But it was more than enough for me, and I just hated Hitler and all of his mob rule from that day.

When the war came to Norway, April 9, 1940, I was fourteen-anda-half years old, but if I had had a chance, I would have joined the poor Norwegian Army and fought against them, because at that time, I looked and felt like an eighteen- or nineteen-year-old boy.

I started at the so-called "Middlesklen" in 1940. This was a school you could go through after you had finished the primary school. This school lasted three years, and at that you were supposed to be old enough to make your own choice, either to continue in the high school or begin to work in the industry or whatever you chose. Anyway, early 1941, I joined a group at the school, and as usual, I was three to four years younger than the others. This group tried to keep up the resistance will among youngsters. *"Hitler siegt an allen fronten"* ("Hitler wins on all front lines"), as the Germans liked to say, and indeed, it did look bad.

We had an enthusiastic teacher as a leader, and we distributed small, illegal papers, showing a clear front against the Nazis. It was a dangerous thing to do, especially after the summer of 1941, because then the Gestapo was established in Larvik as well as all over Norway. In October of 1941, things went wrong. There were about eight or nine pupils, plus one teacher, who were members of Quisling's Nazi party, the Norwegian branch of Hitler's mob. They had found out that something must be going on at the school, and we were caught. We were arrested and sent to the Gestapo. Two were sent to prison and I was kicked out from school and denied all further education at Norwegian schools. First they wanted to send me to prison too, but they found to their surprise that I had not yet reached sixteen—that I would be sixteen two months later. Funny enough, at that time, they still followed Norwegian laws in some strange manner. To end this story, I can tell you that the school's principal smuggled me in the back door the year after that, and with a lot of extra hours in the important school subjects, I graduated from school at the right time in 1943.

Finished with the school, I began to work as a lumberjack. With that kind of work, I could come and go when I wanted to. I was not paid per hour but for how many times I cut. The job was more or less a blind for what I did because I continued to work with illegal things. In 1941, the Germans had confiscated all radios. It was strictly forbidden to listen to news from London or other countries. Well, at that time, we had two radios in the house; we delivered one and kept the other. We had to hide it well, and I built a secret room in the wall in my brother's and my bedroom. As usual, I took the lead, but we had to get news out to the people, so we stole back radios from where the Germans had stored them. We had to do that quite regularly during the whole war because radios at that time were filled up with lamps and pipes, and you could not go to the shop and buy spares. So, when a radio broke down, we had to steal a new one.

We were many groups now, and we listened to the news from London, printed it down, and made some small pamphlets, or as we called them, "illegal newspapers." These had to be brought around to people, and that was the most dangerous part of the work. Germans were everywhere; you never knew when they would stop you and inspect you. Some members of our groups were caught; they were either sent to KZ camps in Germany or executed.

After all, this was only the beginning. In 1943 and 1944, we got weapons from England, and more militant groups took form. Weapons were dropped down from airplanes, were taken care of by the resistance forces, and stored in secret places. It was almost a dispensation of fate that one of these secret places ended up being where I lived. We had a small farm three to four kilometers outside Larvik. Not much of a farm left, but it still had a big barn, and in a barn, you could hide a lot of things—for instance, radios and weapons. My father knew that I did some things not accepted by the Germans. But he preferred not to see things so he stayed away from the barn in the night. During 1944–1945 I became "a darkness man," and I hid all kinds of light weapons, Enfield rifles, Sten guns, Bren guns, hand grenades, and ammunition. They were hidden well because we very often had inspections by the Germans. Four to five kilometers away in Stavern was a German camp for Russian prisoners, and the prisoners now and then would run away. Searching for the fugitives, the Germans, of course, inspected all houses and barns in the neighborhood.

In the last part of the war, January–February, 1945, we had more weapons in the country than we had men to use them. Until that time, I think we had 15,000 to 20,000 people all over the country doing illegal work. We now had to recruit more men, but we had to be careful. Many people could not keep their mouths shut when they should. Anyway, we recruited about 20,000–25,000 men, and when the war ended, we had more than 40,000 men ready to fight. The fact was that the Germans had made Norway into a *Festung Norwegen* (fortress), as they called it, and many fanatic Nazis wanted to keep on with the war even after they had capitulated in "das Vaterland." So we had to be prepared.

I took my two-years-older brother with me to the barn. I had kept him outside, as far as it could be done; only one from a family should deal with illegal work. He was not like me. He was much more rational, not at all that reckless, or maybe I should say "senseless," as I was. When he saw all the weapons I had, he became a bit troubled. But I said to him, "OK, you listen. I have been living on the edge for more than three years. I know that if they get me, I am done for. This way it has to be; there is no going back. Either you are in, or you can stay outside. No one will blame you if you do. But I can sure use your help. I have to teach our new recruits how to use the weapons. Most of them never have seen a gun, not talking about holding a gun and firing it. If you join us, there is no way back."

He did not hesitate, and I gave him a short briefing on how to handle the guns and the ammunition. He took care of that part after that. I was busy with other duties because we received new weapons all the time, and in February of 1945, we started to pass out the weapons to the men who should have them. We had to do that ourselves. As few as possible should know where we had the weapons, so this had to be done in the night.

The new men were mostly "old" people, meaning they were all past thirty to thirty-five years. I was nineteen, so it was not too easy to start "schooling" them. But I looked older, and they believed I was twenty-five or twenty-six years old; I preferred not to tell them my real age.

Anyway, I very seldom talk about the war time. People have asked me if I had any aftereffects from those years. Well, I hadn't been human if I had not. I did have some nightmares after the war, dreaming about situations when it was close; but after some years, these dreams stopped. One little, funny thing I can tell you, I slept with my clothes on in years after, or better to say, I had my best sleep when I kept my clothes on.

Fortunately, the Germans' Chief Commander surrendered the day after Admiral Donitz had signed the capitulation papers in Germany. The resistance

56

forces took over "law and order," I was taken into the police corps in Larvik, and I was there until August of 1945.

I was more or less working with illegal things for three years during World War II. What I did, thousands of others did too. The only thing a little unusual with me was my age. I have not heard of any other boy eighteen or nineteen years old who was responsible for guns enough to fight a little war. But though I was young of age, I looked much older and acted like a man at least ten years older.

I was no hero. None of us were. We just were young men hating this terrible Nazi system. And we wanted to fight against it. In 1945, we were ready, and nobody knew at that time if the Germans would go on fighting in *Festung Norwegen*. There were about 320,000 top-trained German soldiers in Norway when the war ended. Many of them were fanatic Nazis. Fortunately, they decided to surrender two days after the war ended in the rest of Europe. Then we took over law and order. As I said, I was transferred to the police force in Larvik.

We just loved to make the Germans look like fools, and they were so disciplined that they just could not understand our way of thinking. I had a certain contact with the communist-led Saborg. This was the reason: In 1942 and 1943, I had a girlfriend with the name Elsa Bruun. Her brother, Petter, was one of the top men in Saborg, one of the most wanted by the Germans. He and the boss himself, Asbjorn Sunde, were friends from the war in Spain. They had been together there, fighting against Franco. Asbjorn Sunde became a very disputed person, to say it mildly, after the war. But there is no doubt that he was Norway's toughest soldier during World War II, communist or not.

Anyway, I met Petter Bruun sometime in 1942. One way or another, he knew about me and what I was doing. He was at that time wanted by the Gestapo. His picture was all over. He took me aside and said to me, "Arne, whatever you do, don't you ever think about mixing Elsa up with your illegal work. If you do, and something happens to her, I will get you."

I pretended to look like I didn't know what he was talking about, but he just smiled, and his eyes were like ice.

He also said, "If things get too boring for you, just tell me. We can use one like you."

Later on, in 1944, I was contacted by the Saborg leader in Larvik. Before the war, he had been my brother's best friend. They were in the same Labour Party Youngster Union, or whatever you will call it. At that time, I really thought about joining the more active Saborg, but I was stopped.

Chapter 9

LONDON MEMORIES

∞

BENNY MCCOY

I WAS IN a bombing raid my first day in London. Three guys were required to work as fireguards on top of a building to put out fires that day, and I was one of the three. Everybody else ran to the air raid shelter. With the buzz bombs, or V-1s, Germany was trying to pinpoint our short-wave radio station. The station was adjacent to my office.

FRANCIS KNAPP

It seemed like they put us all together on the first floor, packed in one room. They figured the Germans couldn't kill us all, I guess.

BENNY MCCOY

The V-1s had no pilot. They had a motorcycle engine. That's what drove the bombs. The bombs would blow up an entire block. Fireguards used sand on the fires to put them out. Incendiary bombs were dropped on top of buildings to burn holes in them. That means they set the buildings on fire. These bombs caused "flack"—they sent metal in every direction. A V-1 would hit straight down and explode. When the engine cut off, you would know it was coming straight to the earth.

LLOYD POSTEL

The V-1 weapon sounded like a washing machine or motorcycle engine. I never saw a V-1, but I heard them explode.

Years after the war, my wife, Vera, and I went to Washington and saw the National Air and Space Museum. I went up on the mezzanine floor and was looking down, trying to take a picture of the first international space station they had there. A black object kept getting in the way of the camera. Finally, I yanked the camera down and looked up—I could reach out and touch the V-1.

The V-1 was a jet with wings and an explosive charge the Germans launched against England. They flew low, but in London, they were always in the fog, and though I never saw one, they were low enough to hear. They could be aimed to fly over London, at which point they would be sent into a circle over the city until they ran out of fuel, and then they would come down and explode.

If you heard the V-1 once, it wasn't bad. But if you heard the thing the second time, suddenly you were no longer in a city of 8 million. It was now a circle of 360°, and you're in it; and you had better hit the hole. You knew it was going to run out of fuel. And when it did, it was going to come down. If you waited for that, you wouldn't be in the hole in time.

The V-2 was a rocket that was fired to an altitude of about sixty miles, where it also exhausted its fuel and came straight down and exploded. One hit Selfridge's, a big department store, one morning when we sneaked into town (which was off limits). It went through four floors of concrete and steel before exploding. They found ice in some of the holes made by the things, apparently from moisture gathered at great altitude.

BENNY McCOY

You couldn't hear the V-2, yet it did more damage than a V-1 could. Germany bombed London incessantly. The Germans kept trying to find us and bombing where they thought we might be.

There was a faction of people that wanted Winston Churchill to talk with Hitler to end the war. Churchill considered a meeting, but he changed his mind. A meeting wouldn't have worked. Hitler was killing the Jews.

Bombing destroyed the city of London, but it didn't kill the British because they were tough. The French would have quit. The Italians would have too. The Germans didn't stop until they were defeated. Japan could have still made war, but Germany couldn't. They were beaten. All their men at the right age were killed. They had to start relying on older men over forty years old and younger men under eighteen.

LLOYD POSTEL

I have some funny memories of trying to communicate with Londoners. Some Londoners spoke with a *"My Fair Lady"* tone, in a Cockney accent. They never said the "H" and usually dropped other syllables out of words. The first time that I heard a Cockney Londoner speak, I didn't understand a word he said. Their brogue was like nobody else's. I can't say it like they can, but they had an expression, "hapny"—or "a half penny" as we would say.

Margo, a girl I was dating off and on, worked at the other end of the teletype room down at the war room in the English Unit. One day I picked her up to see a movie at Prince of Wales Theater. We took the Underground subway and came out at what we thought was the right station—there were four or five ways to come out. We couldn't tell where we had come out, so she grabbed my arm and said, "Let's go. We'll ask him." There was a guy selling newspapers at the corner. We went over, and she asked him, "Is the Prince of Wales there?"—which was pretty academic.

The newspaper salesman dropped not just Hs but whole syllables. He was pointing and yelling in what might as well have been Greek! Margo thanked him and grabbed my arm, steering me around the corner out of sight by an iron fence. She stopped, looked up at me, and asked, "Now what did he say?"

I said, "You're asking me?"

Margo grew up in Sunderland, one of the most heavily bombed towns during World War II, which was about one hundred miles north of London. This newspaper salesman had spent his entire life in London, and they couldn't communicate! Oh, it was fierce.

"Hapny, hapny, it's an hapny," a collector called as Margo and I stepped onto a double-decker bus. (Phonetically, it's "oipney," The word is "half-penny," but you have to whine it.)

Margo and I went up on the top of the bus and sat down. The conductor came around to collect fares, having what fun he could with Americans who didn't understand. I didn't know what the fare was. He told me how much.

"Two three-oipnies," he said.

"Huh?" I asked.

"Two three-oipnies, please."

I looked blank, he repeated it, and Margo nudged me and said, "Give him two three-oipnies." I had never heard her speak like that.

I made the standard American soldier response—I fished out all the money I had and held it out to the guy. He took a thruppence piece (about a nickel), and I said something like, "That's a thruppence." This brought down the house. The whole busload thought it was hilarious. What they overlooked was that they all understood everything I said, but it didn't work the other way around. The fare was threepence for the two of us, but in addition to the accent problem (dialect almost), they asked for it as "two three-halfpennies, please." The translation of that is: two fares (Margo and me) of three halfpennies each. Whether I would have understood it if he had said "a penny and a half" I don't know, but "one thruppence" I surely would have understood.

Margo was helping me count the money, so I took a standard shot— you grab all the coins and hold them out—two three-half pennies I guess it was.

What he was taking was two thruppence, but he was telling me "two three-hapnies is two half pennies." One and a half and one and a half is three, but only an Englishman would ask for two fares at three hapnies.

And then the whole bus thought that was funny.

Benny and Myrl McCoy with sons, Randall and Darrell

Randall McCoy (on left), Darrell McCoy (on right)

Myrl McCoy, Benny McCoy, Darrell McCoy, Randall McCoy, Angela McCoy (Horn)

Benny McCoy and sister and brother-in law, John and Vera Wall Montgomery

Angela McCoy (one year old)

Benny and Myrl McCoy with daughter, Angela

Benny and Myrl McCoy with granddaughter Cristen Horn, daughter of Angela

Benny McCoy with mother, Arzelia Wall; son Darrell McCoy; and granddaughter Michelle McCoy (Tuttle), Darrell's eldest child

Benny McCoy and grandson Brian McCoy, son of Benny's older son, Randall

Chapter 10

OSS COMMUNICATIONS AT POUNDON HILL

Benny McCoy

How could we have been any luckier than to end up in the OSS?

—Francis Knapp

ANGELA HORN

THE FOLLOWING GROUP discussion between Benny McCoy, Francis Knapp, Lloyd Postel, and Hans Halverson was recorded in Brownsville, Texas, as the men reminisced about their experiences in England, France, and Italy. They began working together in the communications unit of the OSS in a little village they called Poundon—often referred to by them as "Poundon Hill."

BENNY MCCOY

Linny Decunia was older than the rest of us. He had a band, singers, and musicians. He lived club life, drinking and socializing. Decunia was Italian. I met him when I came to Poundon Hill from London. Poundon Hill was a British air force communications center, a broadcasting station that the OSS took over.

"What's your name?" Decunia asked me.

"Benard," I told him.

"OK, my name is Leonard. They call me Linny. We're going to call you Benny."

We could tune in late at night and hear Boston, Massachusetts. It was by accident one night that I picked up Boston. After that, I listened to Boston every time I got the chance. We wanted to hear news from home, not from Europe.

Our station was British and American, and we even had a women's communications detachment. They lived on one side, and we lived on the other. They were daughters of British officers.

There were two other stations, one in the little city of Aylsbury. They would run short of help. I would ride fifteen miles from Poundon to Aylsbury on a bicycle to broadcast to our agents. I'd have to eat lunch there, and I didn't like their food. I was there to help them catch up with their messages to the spies in France and Norway. Mostly women operated the British teletype. They admired my fast typing. They couldn't keep up with the messages and were glad when I came.

JOE LEWIS

My wife had two older brothers, Prentis Morehead and Henry Morehead, who were also stationed in Europe. Henry, stationed in England, wrote me a letter, asking if I would meet him at the Red Cross Club, or the USO, in Oxford. I rode a bicycle about twenty-five miles from Poundon Hill to Oxford. There were quite a few hills. The trip took two to three hours. Joe

Lewis was entertaining the troops at the USO while we were there. He shook our hands and asked how we were doing and how we were being treated.

Joe Lewis was a liaison for the troops. He had a tremendous personality. I had heard about his boxing bouts. No boxing opponent had better step in front of Joe's right hand. He knocked out Max Schmeling in about a minute and a few seconds. Schmeling was a parachute soldier for the Germans.

Henry recalls the incident: "Leslie Denman and Harace McCoy (Benny) drove me to Lufkin, Texas, on April 11, 1943. The next day, I caught the bus for Fort Leonardwood, Missouri, where I enlisted in the Army Air Force in engineering. I was in boot camp there for about six weeks, came home for two weeks, left for New York, and stayed until September 12, 1943. I left New York for Liverpool, England, and arrived five or six days later. I was stationed in Huntingdon, England, about six months. About six months later, while stationed in Barrington Park, England, I wrote Harace a letter. We set up a day to meet in Oxford. Several guys and I got together and drove to Oxford and met up with Harace. There were guys everywhere. Harace and some other guys and I were sitting at a table, and in walked Joe Lewis. He came to our table and shook our hands, talked a little, just mainly trying to boost up our morale. Joe's neck was as big as his head. I'll never forget that."

COMMUNICATIONS

When I was recruited into the OSS, I was taught how to kill a man with my bare hands and not make a sound in case I did not have a weapon. I drew military wages and wore a military uniform, but I actually performed OSS duties that were separate from the military. The address I used was "OSS Detachment, APO 887, New York, New York." The title "OSS Detachment" meant that I was detached from the military. I expedited messages on the air and into people's hands. My title, Communications Clerk, was kept as anonymous as possible. Communications reported directly to General William Donovan, "Wild Bill," the director of OSS. Few people actually knew where my office was located or what type of work I did. They might have been aware that somebody was encoding and decoding information but not where the information was coming from. Those who did know were aware of the exact origin where messages were encoded and decoded. These people included Allen Dulles, the OSS representative in Switzerland, and his superior, William J. Donovan, head of the OSS.

Knapp, Postel, Halverson, Brunette, Clark, and I were selected to decode and encode secret and top-secret messages to different locations and people in Communications. We did the same type of work but usually worked different shifts, and we worked at the most powerful short-wave radio station in the world. "Poundon Hill," as we called it, was near Bicster, a little town not far from London. Three stations were spaced about a mile apart. One was live, and the other two were bogus. The live station was located near a sweet shop and a theater. We worked at the live station. I frequented both places. Like I said, we could hear broadcasts from a station in Boston, Massachusetts. We enjoyed listening to what was happening on the home front. Though we wanted to converse with the Boston station, we were not allowed to.

As foot soldiers in intelligence, we communicated the intent of the American leaders to the spies behind the lines and vice versa. The spies informed us of the intent of the German military plans, which were in turn forwarded to the Allies' leadership, basically officers in England, America, France, and Free Europe.

Captain Williams, the commandant over the entire operation of Communications at the radio station, was loved by all of us. He was everybody's friend. If you had any problem in administration, he would take care of it. He was not one to gripe, and he was kind.

Men and women ate in the mess hall. The agents that were to be dropped by air behind the lines to help with the resistance army in Europe often ate with us at night. Most of them spoke two or three languages. They were always dropped at night with ample equipment and supplies. We were not allowed to ask them their names. They were a happy-go-lucky bunch. One group that went through Poundon Hill didn't stay happy-go-lucky for long, however. Francis remembers what happened to them.

FRANCIS KNAPP

Fourteen guys came through our office. When they were dropped, they were caught and killed because somebody in their group was German and was a "crossover"—someone who had gone through the course with them.

BENNY MCCOY

One night it was drizzling when the defend-the-camp signal sounded. It was a training session. Francis said, "Benny, let's not fall out tonight; let's not get out in this. Let's just camouflage ourselves so we can't be seen. You get in that chifferobe, and I will pull this blanket off of the bottom of this bed so that it comes onto the floor. I'll roll under that, and we won't go out."

Horns were blowing, making all kinds of fuss outside. Usually it didn't last too long, but this one went on and on. People were coming through the barracks and sounding alarms. We didn't know what was going on.

I had to squat down in the chifferobe, which cut the circulation off in my legs. My head began to pound, and I thought, *I've got to get out of here; I'm about to black out.* So I began to hit the door on the chifferobe. I couldn't move my legs. I couldn't even feel them. As I shoved against the back of the chifferobe, I fell out onto the floor.

Knapp heard me and came out from under the bed saying, "What is going on?"

I said, "I've lost all the feeling in my legs. If they come in here and catch me, we're in trouble."

We hid out and didn't go to defend the camp that night. They had been hunting us but didn't catch us. If we would have been caught, we probably would have been put on kitchen police (KP) duty for a week. Occasionally on Sundays, I would pull KP duty for a certain friend. He would pay me $5.00.

A guy came in our camp one day, about six-feet, four-inches tall, and Lloyd Postel, who was a bundle of energy, said, "There's a monster in the camp." Lloyd was six-feet, *five,* inches tall! The bunks were not long enough for Lloyd or "the monster," as Lloyd called him, and Lloyd found a box to give himself extra space to sleep.

Lloyd Postel

The box was a drawer out of a dresser. Barracks B-13 was a Nissen hut, a half circle of corrugated metal. The bunks were British Army issue, and they were midgets—each a two-by-four rectangle that was five feet, six inches long and about two-and-a-half feet wide. They put metal straps (like the kind that hold a cardboard box or an old, orange crate together) from side to side and end to end. Then you took a mattress cover or a cotton sack, filled it with straw, and put it down on the metal straps. It was uncomfortable for anybody, but trying to squeeze six feet, four inches onto a five-feet, six-inch frame was unthinkable. I "liberated" a drawer from a desk or dresser, folded an army blanket into several layers of thickness over it, and then rammed the double bunk against the end of B-13 to hold the drawer (on the edge) and the blanket. Then I put a pillow or another folded army blanket on it. This way I could sleep with my head on the extension made with the drawer and my shoulder rammed up against the end, two-by-four, of the bunk. Even then, I had to sleep in an S position.

71

I have to tell this story about Benny, Francis, and me. Francis had the upper bunk, and Benny had the lower one. Knapp took his liner out of his helmet and filled it with lukewarm water. Benny's hand was dangling, so Knapp put Benny's hand in the liner. Next thing you know, Benny was wetting the bed. He came roaring out of the sack! Knapp went banging through the door. There was no getting him back. He figured Benny was going to kill him.

A week or two went by, and I got a proposition from Benny. "You've got to help me get even," he said.

Knapp slept without any clothes on. He was naked under the army blanket. Benny and I knew how to take the bunks apart. We carried Knapp, still asleep in his bunk, wrapped up in his army blanket, out where the English gals went by to the common mess hall. There Francis stayed—naked under the blanket—until one of the officers began yelling, "Get that man out of here!" Knapp was yelling at us to come help him. As far as I can remember, we refused so that he would have to walk back with his blanket. The whole camp was laughing about the incident, even the officers.

LLOYD POSTEL

The OSS experience was like college, I think, mostly because of the demographics. Our group was made up of all college kids in one way or another. So we felt very comfortable with whichever one of us was available to pal around with when we weren't working. The shifts would change in a way that we all would work together. Different combinations of two or three guys would be off at the same time.

What was important to the OSS wouldn't occur to you or me. They had strange priorities. The OSS had a different way of doing everything. I remember the old saying, "There's a right way, and there's an Army way," but the OSS had still a third way.

One guy, Tony, hated Frank Sinatra like a poison. They had both started in the same nightclub somewhere in New Jersey. Tony sang opera. Sinatra was popular and making millions in Hollywood while Tony was overseas shouting orders at us.

There were no guys who wound up in prison or on drugs. The OSS was somewhat selective, but that's not the proof of anything either. Normally, in a military unit you're going to expect problems along with everybody else. But this one had no problems in it, with one exception—a guy who had the foulest mouth I'd ever heard.

Benny McCoy

One guy with us at Poundon, whose dad worked for International Telephone and Telegraph (IT&T), had a lot of money. He would make a stack of pounds when he gambled. He would roll the dice, throwing those pounds out there. He came to a ten shilling note once, which was half a pound. He grabbed that, threw it away, and said, "How'd that get in there?"

I didn't gamble. Most of the other guys didn't have much more than a couple of dollars to spend, so their gambling amounted to a Dominos game, taking nickels away.

Near the teletype room and the message center was a room we didn't use except as a junk room to store things. We put our clothes in a little chest of drawers there. And each of us had a shelf that we kept our writing materials on. A new guy came in one day, walked back there, and began to pull the stuff out of that drawers and off the shelves. He began to sling the things across that junk room. One of the guys, Kelly, walked in about that time. Kelly lost himself at this guy and hit him between the hips and the knees, just like he was tackling on a football field, and they went down. That was the most excitement I ever saw in that office.

We had a lot of comers and goers there, people we didn't even know. Tony [the officer Lloyd mentioned] only knew how to sing. He was impossible. All he wanted to do was groom himself, look handsome, and sing.

Lloyd Postel

He was in charge of a unit and didn't know how to work with anyone. He couldn't direct anything, but he was obligated by the position to do it, and it made him nervous. He was twitchy.

Benny McCoy

Lloyd, I think you did make a little speech that day about organization. You probably don't even remember it. We needed somebody to speak up. I was the youngest one there. I had been called in before the signal master and made to look like a turkey. I knew I could type. I didn't know very much else, but I knew I could type. The signal master asked Tony that day, "What's your purpose for having them in here?" And I remember Tony saying, "Lieutenant, I'm supposed to be supervising a group of men that have grown old enough to be responsible in their jobs, and it's as though I have a bunch of kindergarten kids."

I thought, *Now this guy is calling us a bunch of kindergarteners, and look at himself.* But you answered him when he said that. I've forgotten exactly what you said, but you said something to him that made a lot of sense.

LLOYD POSTEL

I think Tony was in way over his head. He couldn't do the work we did, but he was in charge of making us do it. He didn't understand it. It was this way all the time.

BENNY McCOY

His biggest problem was his inability to like people.

LLOYD POSTEL

He couldn't get over the fact that he got the dirty end of the stick in that nightclub in New Jersey with Frank Sinatra. They had been singing in the same nightclub in New Jersey, right outside New York somewhere. Sinatra was in Hollywood making movies, and Tony was in charge of us.

HANS HALVERSON

Tony thought he should have been in the movies instead of Sinatra.

LLOYD POSTEL

He convinced himself that he was better than Sinatra with singing, and he may have been. I don't think that Frank Sinatra could do "The Donkey Serenade" as well as Tony.

BENNY McCOY

The last I heard of Tony was that he was ill and in an institution because his wife, who was a model, ran around on him, and he lost his mind. If he ever became successful with his singing talent, I never heard.

PROCESSING FIELD COMMUNICATIONS IN CODE
LLOYD POSTEL

The messages from the agent in the field came in dots and dashes in Morse code. Then we would send it by landline to London. A radio operator who communicated it to our office received the message first. We would then send it to the war room. So there was a break, an interruption in the system, a couple of times between the agent in the field and the war room in London. The agents signed their messages with their code names. However, a code name would have no impact except a little in the war room in London. Those in the war room didn't care about the agent's name. They wanted to know the location of the railroad line or whatever else the field agent was watching so that they could correlate intelligently what the agents were picking up.

The code system was drafted to limit the agents to short messages, one hundred words or less, so that they would not be "on the air" any longer than necessary. The field agents always transmitted in Morse code, dots and dashes, not with teletype. The agent would cease transmission at one hundred words and run. Then the field agent would have to shut the machine down and go because the Germans would determine the location of the Morse code transmission. They did not have to break the code or read the message. They simply had to use beams to determine where the field agent was when sending the message. Mostly, the field agent would be on a hillside overlooking a French railroad line, counting boxcars and using field glasses to see their contents as best he could. Then he'd code the message into five letter groups and make it no longer than one hundred of them to limit transmission time and to tell us in England what he saw, and then he'd run. The Germans would pinpoint his location from the radio transmission and start after him before he finished it. These were quickies. If you got enough quickies together, you could obtain a sensible message.

The inventor of the typewriter designed a keyboard that is still used on the computer today. It's the same keyboard, A-S-D-F, that whole routine, and it never changed. For shorthand, there were several different versions. But with typing, there was just one keyboard. Vera, my wife, had a German typewriter for a while, and it had the same typical keyboard.

During World War II, when you think about it, it was fairly rare to find a guy who could type. Now, every kid has to know how. He can't go through school without a computer.

BENNY McCOY

Colonel Rudishand, my boss in Paris, would instruct the cryptographers, those who operated the code machines: "If you take a message, break it down, type it, and send it to its recipient. If it's top secret and has to do with anything that the Germans might find out, you don't have a right to show that to another person in the room. If you show that to someone else, you're subject to court martial."

To begin to operate the coding machine, it had to first fit into a teletype machine. I would plug the coding machine into the teletype machine, type the message in English, and it would come out in French. I decoded it and then typed in a teletype that would say "Eyes Only," a military term meaning that it went to the highest authority. Messages often went to Eisenhower at SHAEF and Chief of Staff, George C. Marshall, in Washington, D.C., who covered all the US military in the world.

A lot of incoming messages could result in tapes from the machine filling the floor. Coded tapes hung all around the teletype room. In the Poundon Hill office, the agents in Communications would usually type for eight hours and sometimes an extra two to four hours. However, when I went to Paris, there were times I typed messages for sixteen hours straight.

SIGTOT MACHINES

The Sigtot machines were electric machines. Our OSS short-wave radio station was located at Poundon Hill. Two more stations were located between Poundon Hill and London. The major operation was at Baker Street in London, and that office controlled all the other radio operations. We had secondhand machines compared to them. They overshadowed us at Poundon Hill and had seniority over us when it came to operations. They had more control over top-secret information than what we had. The Poundon Hill station was operated by Americans until they brought a contingent of British soldiers and WAAFS in. The WAAFS operated two of the stations. Often, I would go over to their stations and type all day to help them catch up. Their work had to do with the British intelligence.

Benny McCoy playing solitaire

Benny McCoy

Benny McCoy in snow

Chapter 11

BENNY, FRANCIS, AND HANS IN PARIS, FRANCE

ജ

Tommy Lowndes, Hans Halverson, Benny McCoy

Benny McCoy by barbed wire outside Paris OSS office near LIDO Club

Benny McCoy by barbed wire outside Paris

Francis Knapp by barbed wire outside Paris

HANS HALVERSON

I THINK THE plan was to drop me into Norway while the Germans were there, but before I finished the course at the University of Wisconsin, the Germans were out of Norway. Some of us were sent to Washington, D.C. From there, they sent me to the London OSS office, where I spent some time and then went on to Paris. This is when I met my lifelong friends.

I have one small incident I should tell you about. I was sent from Paris to London and had to go to the Orly Field to catch an army plane. The weather was not good, so they did not let any plane take off until it got a little better. While waiting around for the weather to change, I sat next to a man whom I had a conversation with. The man I was talking to was the popular orchestra director Glenn Miller. He signed a French franc for me that I've kept. I was probably the last person to talk to him. The weather cleared, and I got on the army plane. Glenn Miller had his own private plane. He went down between Paris and London that day and was never heard from again.

BENNY McCOY

I remember hearing the Glenn Miller band would be performing in Paris, and I went. Tex Beneke was in charge that night. He said, "Major Miller is coming later, on another flight." But Glenn Miller never made it. There are two possible theories. One was that an American pilot dumped bombs over the English Channel instead of over Berlin and that the bombs hit Major Miller's plane. The other theory was that the plane iced over on the wings and crashed. My opinion lies with either of these theories.

The OSS sent me to Paris after D-Day had passed. The Germans had been pushed out. Paris had been liberated. Francis Knapp, Richard Ziegler, and I left Poundon, spent the night in London, got up the next morning, and went to the airport. A C47 transported us from London to Paris. Hans Halverson and Al Clark were bumped from that flight. Francis and I sat on the left side of the C47. It was raining, and Francis worried because every time the plane would hit a cloud, it would bounce up and down. He would say, "I wonder if that wing is going to fall off."

When we landed at the airport in Paris (the same one where Charles Lindbergh had landed in 1927), we were put into an old jalopy with our luggage. The driver dropped us off on a sidewalk. None of us could speak a word of French. We couldn't understand a thing he was saying. He couldn't speak a word of English. We got off and said, "We don't know where to go." We had an address but didn't even know where we were. We agreed that somebody would have to go look for the address and somebody would have to stay with the luggage.

"Well, let's me and somebody go look for the address," Francis said.

Francis didn't want to be by himself. He never wanted to be alone. I said, "Well, you guys go ahead and find this place while I guard the luggage. I've got my .45. I'm armed, but don't you guys stay gone all day and night. Don't leave me here by myself." They stayed and stayed. I decided they were lost. People came and went.

A little boy about eight or nine years old came by and said, "Hi, Yank."

I said, "Hi. Where did you learn to speak English?"

He said, "I took it in school. What are you doing out here alone with all of these bags?"

I said, "I'm here on a mission, and I'm looking for the place I'm supposed to go."

"What's the address?"

I read the address to him: "79 Champs-Élysées."

He said, "I'll take you there. I know exactly where it is."

I said, "But you can't carry this luggage. It's too heavy for you."

He said, "I'll get somebody to watch part of it, and I'll go show you the place. We'll come back and get the other. I'll help you do it." He was a sharp little boy. We began to move that stuff, and here came Knapp and Ziegler. Ziegler and Knapp said, "We found the place."

I said, "You've been gone for two hours. I didn't go anywhere but stayed right here and found it." The place was on the widest avenue in Paris, des Champs-Élysées, south of the Arc de Triomphe, and on another side of the office was Avenue Victor Hugo.

Processing Messages in the Paris OSS Office

All five stories of the building in which I worked in Paris belonged to the OSS. The building was guarded twenty-four hours per day. The guards were armed with .45 automatics and rifles. The only access to the building was an elevator. The stairwell was completely sealed off with doors. Only the guards could allow access through the stairs.

A military generator supplied all of our electricity. The generator was located on the street next to our building and was placed on a military transport. Iron posts that sank into the ground secured it. In a room on the fifth floor, there was a large window on the street side, where the OSS equipment and top-secret materials were housed. The balcony outside that window was completely covered with barbed wire, preventing entrance by any shape, form, or fashion. That made our room secure. Nobody could get to us. The generator was beneath this barbed wire on the street level.

The entrance to our OSS office was at the back of the Lido Club, known as the most famous nightclub in the world, on the Champs-Élysées, one of the most famous streets in the world. The Lido Club had front and side entrances. The front entrance on the Champs-Élysées side had an attractive glass window and glass doors. The Lido Club was like the 21 Club in Washington D.C. The club had a large foyer where there were elevators. While I waited for the elevator one day, Major General William Donovan ("Wild Bill") appeared through the side entrance of the Lido Club with an entourage of officers. There must have been a dozen of them. They came up to our office. As Donovan walked into the office, he shook hands with everybody, giving us all high-fives and words of encouragement, such as, "You're doing a good job." While in our office, he looked over our teletype and code machines.

Donovan was President Roosevelt's personal friend. Roosevelt didn't ask for permission from Congress but formed the OSS and placed Donovan over it. Part of my job was to get messages out *tout de suite*, which meant immediately or right away. The job required speed in typing. Hunt-and-peck typing never would have gotten the job done.

In OSS Communications, rank meant nothing. Sergeants worked under me. Francis Knapp was the night supervisor, and I was the day supervisor. Not even the assistant supervisors could know messages that we received or sent.

Reutershan, my boss in Paris, told me personally, "When you get a message in here and it's from an agent, you get a message and you decipher it. You don't show that to anybody else in this room. You put that right through this message center and get it out of here because you don't know what that other guy might tell about you. If I hear of you passing that message around for others to read, I will court martial you." It really scared me, and I don't doubt that he would have done it.

Richard (Dick) Ziegler was the first sergeant over administrative procedures and oversaw food, clothing, mail, medical, and similar details. Dick was a member of the OSS but did not have access to the transmission of top-secret information. The lieutenant junior grade (JG) in the Navy who was our superior in Paris was a young guy, not dry behind the ears. He was under a Navy lieutenant who was under Colonel Reutershan. Only Army people were our bosses in Paris—no Navy people were over us.

Eventually, we stopped going to the Petit Palace to sleep because of inclement weather. Instead, we slept in the building where our office was. The two stories immediately below us were unoccupied, and we put cots on some of those floors. Because of this, Al Clark and I were listed once as AWOL. Our Paris superior put out a notice on us. I showed the notice to Ziegler and said, "You've got to get me out of trouble. They've got a deal posted down at the Petit Palace that I'm AWOL."

Ziegler took the listing down to the administration and had us taken off of the list. He told them, "He's working in top secret stuff. He's not AWOL. We know where he is."

INVASION OF FRANCE

Do you know what a battleship can do? It can shoot a shell sixty miles. It can tear everything up for thirty miles. When we invaded France, it didn't matter that we were the invaders. We had 5,000 ships in the English Channel. There were battleships, aircraft carriers, and LSTs (landing ship tanks). Those battleships sat there all day and all night and shot those big guns, and they tore that place up. The people who lived through the invasion were so shell-shocked that they didn't even know their names. Many of them couldn't even walk—the shocks from shells exploding made them act like they were drunk. The bigger guns on the English side bombarded the German forces in France. Many hit obstacles. Some landed in ponds. It was a mess. We had to get on the mainland of Europe to win the war, and that was the only way we could get there. If you are going to war, you have to make your mind up to die. When we boarded that ship to go to Europe, they told us, "Prepare to die."

FIGHTING A LOST CAUSE

It seemed impossible to Germany that an army could cross the English Channel and land on the shores of France. These shores had been made impregnable. It was thought that no army could come ashore. They were not aware of the powerful firepower of the United States Army. They were unaware of the tremendous determination of the British people. So they sat behind their fortifications, thinking they could throw us back into the sea.

Rommel, the greatest tank man the Germans ever produced, got in his staff car and went home for the weekend. The weather forecasters had assured him there would be no invasion that weekend. He took his aide, who chauffeured him back into the heart of Germany so he could see his wife. Back there in the heart of Germany, June 6, it was late in the day before anyone

85

notified him that the invasion was taking place. A few days before, Rommel had been talking about the invasion, that the day the Allies invaded France would be the longest day of the war. He knew it would be a fight to the finish. The Germans felt sure they would be strong enough to throw the amphibious forces back into the sea. Rommel was so sure we would not invade at that time that he left his forces.

Rommel was the one chosen by Hitler to keep the Americans and the British from invading France, but he left matters in the hands of aides and went home. He had the respect of the American army. Yet, before he could get back to Saint Lowe and the area being invaded, it was too late. Those amphibious forces had landed men on top of men. Thousands had died, and others had dug in. Glider troops had landed behind the lines, and paratroopers had been dropped. The beachhead had been secured. All the fire power that Germany could get to it was not enough. Twenty-seven thousand American planes flew over those shores, dropping bombs and shooting and strafing—shooting from low-flying aircraft using 20-millimeter cannons and/or machine guns. When it was cloudy, the enemy couldn't strafe due to limited vision.

Ten thousand American men died on the beaches that day, taking the first step in the fall of Hitler and his maniacal ideas of conquering the world. The Nazis might have succeeded, but they made some mistakes. They didn't know they were coming up against a force more powerful than they were or that they were fighting for a lost cause. Had they known the weaknesses of the invasion force, they probably could have thrown us back into the sea. But they were unaware of any weaknesses in the invasion force.

The greatest armada of ships that has ever been assembled on the seas of this world since the beginning of time was on the English Channel that morning. The American sailors and British sailors climbed up those ropes, ran across those beaches, and fought their way into the interior, pushing the Germans back and fighting into the hedgerows.

There was one incident of a German captain who kept a group of men in a bunker that had only one door to the outside. The Americans could not get them out. The Germans knew they were being encircled, but the captain refused to let them out. So the Americans brought up a weapon they had called a "flamethrower." They turned it on that bunker, and it got so hot inside that the men's flesh began to cook and burn. The captain still thought they could push us back into the sea. He felt like they couldn't give up and let us stay ashore.

The underground army in France, the Maquis, was supposed to rise up when we landed to unload our glider infantries, but the Maquis ran into problems. However, the Maquis helped to shorten the war.

Some also believe the war was shortened a year because of the OSS. Our founder, Donovan, went to Yugoslavia disguised as a hoodlum, taking about ninety people with him to instigate riots. No one recognized him there. Hitler told Mussolini to bring the Italians in to stop the riots. The Italians went in, but the riots were too much for them to deal with. When Mussolini and the Italians were unsuccessful, Hitler became angry. Donovan's mission caused a delay in Hitler's plan to invade Russia so that when his forces did invade, they were too late because the winter was so severe that it froze the grease in the bearings of their military vehicles. He couldn't proceed any further until the following spring thaw. By then, the US had replenished Russia's military defense so that Germany couldn't take Russia.

When I went overseas, I was promoted first to PFC—private first class—and then to corporal. We didn't feel very first class! All a PFC has is one stripe. Stationed in Paris mostly, I was required to know French, or at least to be able to read it well. I learned French by going to the movies. Paris was full of movies in both French and English.

Sometimes Germans blew our lines up. On those occasions, I either drove a military jeep to deliver a message or called the motor pool for a driver to take me to deliver it. We'd call their number, and they would come in a jeep. Always armed with an M-1 rifle on these missions, I delivered messages to a military top secret courier to be delivered to the war zone or to General Eisenhower. Often Germans killed Americans and then got their uniforms so they could impersonate them in the war. So when the Germans blew our lines up, we could let no one stop us when delivering the message to a military courier.

I didn't know my destinations when a driver would take me to deliver messages. One night, it was raining. I couldn't keep up with which road we were on. It was confusing. Another time, I picked up a secret pouch to deliver to somebody. I tried to forget things. I didn't want to remember. Some things are hard to forget, though, like the two German bombs that were dropped by my building in Paris.

I remember one incident when an American soldier received the command to bomb a particular place. After bombing it, he decided to bomb another place nearby. Many Germans were killed at the second place, but so were several of our spies. Consequently, the soldier was demoted and sent back to the US.

For a while in Paris, I could get news by shortwave radio. The news commentator was hidden underneath turnip greens in a trailer. He had to constantly move, because otherwise, he would have been caught. The commentator and the driver of the turnip green carrier operated by codes. The turnip green salesman let him know when it was time to sell turnip greens again.

BOB HOPE, THE SOLDIER'S FRIEND

Bob Hope came to Paris about the time the war was ending to entertain the troops. One day I was walking west on the Champs-Élysées, along the sidewalk from the place I slept toward my office and walked right into Bob Hope. He was walking in the opposite direction with a lady on his arm (I suppose it was his wife). I was elated and said, "If this isn't a treat for a soldier a long way from home to meet an old friend named Bob Hope on the Champs-Élysées."

He laughed and shook my hand and asked, "G.I., what's your name?"

"I'm Benny McCoy from Texas," I said. "I'm glad to see you."

He patted me on the back and talked about entertaining the troops and what a privilege he considered it to be. Nobody had noticed him until I did. By that time, however, everyone passing by had noticed him. Within a few minutes, a crowd had gathered.

Bob Hope was a soldier's friend. He had a heart for men who were away from home, men who had left their homes to defend a nation. The man was patriotic. He knew how lonely the soldiers could become. When he came to see us, it was like receiving a letter from home.

SIGHTSEEING WITH FRIENDS

Leslie Denman, my best friend from Huntington, Texas, contacted me in Paris. He was chauffeuring a high official somewhere in Germany. He told me what day he was coming through Paris and asked, "You got a place I can stay?"

I said, "Yeah."

He said, "I want to stay a few days with you in Paris." He had a command car with markings on it. We used that command car to go around and see all the sights. We went up and down the Seine, and sometimes we walked on a walkway along the river. Other times, we rode the subway when seeing different attractions in Paris. There was a cathedral up on the hill in Montmartre, a neighborhood on the north side of Paris, where you could get paintings made. Hans got his picture painted in Pigalle. Everybody called it "Pig Alley."

EISENHOWER JACKETS

When the Eisenhower jackets came out, Hans said, "Benny, let's go over to the officer's club and get our Eisenhower jackets."

I said, "How are we going to get our Eisenhower jackets?"

He said, "Well, the officers can buy them. We can't buy them. We'll go over to the officers' club. When they come along, we'll salute them and ask them if they'll buy us one."

I tried it a few times, and I couldn't get anybody to buy me one. Hans tried it, and he didn't either, so we left and went back.

The next day, he said, "Let's go back over to that club."

I said, "No, I'm not going back over there."

Hans said to the first guy he saluted, "Sir, I want you to buy me one of those Eisenhower jackets."

The guy said, "I don't think I'm supposed to do that."

Hans said to me, "You know what I started to tell him?"

I said, "No telling."

Hans replied, "I started to tell him, 'Well, Lieutenant, do you do everything you're told to do?'"

Hans persuaded an officer to buy him one. He got the first one. Knapp and I still had those old blouses. The supply sergeant told us if we'd pay for the jackets, he'd get each of us one. That's when I got mine. I forget what we paid for them. We bought our own before they were issued. Everybody wanted one.

A TRIP TO NICE

With my Class A OSS Pass, I could go anywhere in France.

We were given seven days off on one particular occasion, so I asked Hans, "Where are we going to go?"

He said, "Let's go to the Riviera. The train goes from here to there. We'll just go out here and catch the train to the Riviera."

I said, "OK." We got on the train. Soldiers could ride free of charge.

There was a black guy who got on the train with us. We got down in the Alps, and the train pulled off on a sidetrack there. I don't know if they were waiting for another train or not, but we sat there for an hour.

89

Somebody said, "There's a fruit orchard." It was back in the mountains. The black guy went out in that fruit orchard and gathered a bunch of fruit. He asked Hans and me if we wanted some.

I asked, "Where are you getting the fruit?"

He said, "I'm getting it out of that fruit orchard. I'll go back and get some more."

Whenever the train would stop, I was afraid to get off because I didn't want the train to take off without me. However, our black friend wasn't afraid to, so he would go get drinks for Hans and me. Once he got off at a peach orchard, where the soldiers devoured the peaches from the trees. I said, "Man, this train may leave before you get back. We're up here in these Alps. If you get left, you'll be in trouble."

He said, "Ah, they'll wait 'til I get back." He went up there and gathered a bunch more fruit, and we ate fruit all the way to Nice. He was amazed that we were friendly to him.

We reached Nice, and we wanted to go out further. We weren't just interested in walking around on sand there. Hans and I went on some pedal boats. The coast guard was making a circle three miles out, so Hans and I pedaled out in the blue Mediterranean. The coast guard said, "Get back toward that beach. You don't go any further than this."

Hans would stay in the pedal boat, and I would dive and swim. Then Hans would take his turn at diving and swimming while I stayed in the pedal boat. We wouldn't both leave that pedal boat because we were two miles out from shore. We had to keep the pedal boat to get back to shore.

It was right where Edward had abdicated at his home on the shore. He was the Prince of Wales at that time.

FIDELITY AND FREEZING TEMPERATURES

In Paris, absolutely everything went on. In the area I had to walk from where I slept to where I worked, women would approach me. I had to jerk their hands off me. I was a young soldier in the middle of war with a prestigious job, and I owed it to my government not to contaminate myself. I owed it to the job I had. A little piece of plastic could get me anywhere in any echelon of the military because of who I was and the job that I did. Do you think I was going to contaminate myself with trash that would bring degradation on my head, on my family, and on my young wife back home? I'm not crazy. I've got better sense than that!

Hans and I often talked because we enjoyed mutual things. I always enjoyed listening to him. He would talk for hours about his dad and mom and the things that they did, like planting their wheat field.

One memory I have of Hans in Paris comes to my mind: It's cold, and we don't have any heat in the building where we work. We're trying to type. The engine is not running downstairs. Fingers are cold. We are wearing extra clothes to keep warm. He's telling me, "You know, I can remember back in North Dakota it would be cold. We'd come down, start the car, turn the switch on the car, and that Chevrolet, when it would turn over the first time, would catch and run. You would turn the warm heater on and warm the car and go wherever you went."

Perhaps because of my long working hours in the cold, I was hospitalized with a severe throat infection for two weeks of the ten months I was in Paris.

Another memory of a cold, wintry night was when I was returning with Todd Henrikson, a friend and American soldier of Norwegian descent, from a meeting with a banker who worked for the Bank of France. We were walking on the sidewalk of a dark street when a woman met us and told us to not walk on the sidewalk but to walk in the middle of the street because we were in danger. We had on GI overcoats. It was dark, and the subway wasn't running. We walked the rest of the way in the middle of the street until we could catch the subway.

I also went to Belgium with Henrikson. When Belgium changed their money, all people with old Belgium money had to go to Brussels to change the old for the newly issued Belgium money. Everyone was notified of the day to change the money. The OSS guys decided that Henrikson and I would take the old money that the employees of the OSS had to Brussels to be exchanged. When we arrived in Brussels, we stayed at a hotel one night and met with the Bank of Belgium the next morning to exchange the money. Henrikson and I were given permits to exchange the money.

Once I had an opportunity to go to Switzerland, but lack of money kept me from going. Switzerland was a free country, and anybody's money could be exchanged there. Janet, a US Army WAC, told me she and her boyfriend, an army pilot, flew to Switzerland when they were off duty. They would buy watches there and mail them from Switzerland to the US.

One night Henrikson was picked up by the MPs. He was carrying tools to repair Sigtot machines. The MPs escorted him to police headquarters for further questioning. He was not allowed to reveal what the tools were used for. They kept him for several hours, grilling him with questions. They found his

OSS identification card in his pocket. They contacted their superiors, who let them know that Henrickson was a good spy.

THE RED CROSS

I knew one soldier who received false teeth from his family. He showed me a pocket full of false teeth. The dentists would pay him an enormous amount for them, even up to $1,000. This soldier tried to convince me to also sell false teeth. He was telling me that I could buy false teeth for $200 and sell them for $1,000.

I replied, "No, no. Not $200. I wouldn't take $1,000." I didn't want anything to do with that.

One day, several of us G.I.s were told that the Red Cross was going to serve free coffee and donuts and make photographs of the soldiers. We were on our way to the Red Cross on Place de la Madelaine Rue, and we met half a dozen prostitutes that were hungry and wanted to sell themselves for money to buy food. One of the beautiful girls approached me, and I declined her offer. However, I instructed her to go to the military café on Champs-Élysées and apply for washing dishes, and they would give her a free meal.

We went on to the Red Cross club, and I had a photograph taken that I sent home to my wife. She had a photograph taken also and took her picture and mine to a photography shop and had the two pictures combined into one so that it looked like we had the picture made at the same time. That was her favorite picture. I made two pictures that day, one with my cap on and one with the cap off.

AUSTRIAN CROWN JEWELS

An officer came to our Paris office one day with a box. The box had a wax seal on it, and it had a code. We were instructed to keep that box until someone with the matching code came for it. The box was large enough to sit on and became a piece of our furniture. It stayed there for a while after the war ended.

Later, after I had left Paris, I recall Francis Knapp telling me about the day the military police came to our office with the matching code. They said, "We've come after the box. It's probably not a secret. The newspapers will publish it shortly. It's the Austrian crown jewels." We had been sitting on that box for a long time and didn't even know that it contained the famous Austrian crown jewels.

(According to Kenneth Alford's book *Treasure Stories of World War II*, there were counterfeit artifacts—Holy Crown, scepter, and orb—which ended up in Los Angeles, California, in January of 1946 that are now displayed in the National Infantry Museum, Fort Benning, Georgia).[7]

V-E DAY IN PARIS

During the V-E Day Paris parade, I went up to the balcony of the OSS building and shot pictures as the troops moved on down the Champs-Élysées. I went down into the street after they marched out and took another picture.

Vehicles were coming between the troops, and Eisenhower was standing and waving in one of the vehicles. Churchill was in the other one—with the cigar. He always had a cigar. He was giving everybody the "V" sign, you know, in victory.

Newsweek printed a cover story on Churchill, a resumé on his life and what he meant to the world. They painted him up as being one man that saved the world from Hitler. That's going a long way because Hitler, if he would have taken a little bit of time, would have been able to conquer the world because he would have had the atom bomb; but he was in too big of a hurry. When he blew it on the atomic bomb, he could not overcome the West.

NEWS OF PRESIDENT ROOSEVELT'S DEATH

We were sitting outside the message center, waiting to go to work, when Roosevelt died. One of the workers in the message center said, "Hey, McCoy, listen to this: 'President Franklin D. Roosevelt died at Warm Springs, Georgia, at 3:30 Eastern Standard time today.'"

93

It was 11:58 right then. It lacked two minutes of being midnight because I was to go to work at midnight.

The worker continued, "Harry S. Truman has been sworn in as President of the United States. Who in the hell is Harry S. Truman?"

"He's the vice president," I told him.

"Well, I didn't know who the vice president was."

That shows you how when you're off to war, you might not know what is going on back home in politics. The next morning, when I went to breakfast, the French newspapers were stacked up high where we ate. There were stacks upon stacks up and down the sidewalks. I'm sure there were 100 French people on their knees praying and crying. They came to us, asking, "What is going on?"

I answered them, "Roosevelt *del mort*" (Roosevelt has died), and explained that we're not tied to one man. "We have a constitution to go by. One man died—another will take his place."

Benny McCoy

Benny McCoy

Benny McCoy at Place de Etoile, Paris, 1945, Arc de Triomphe

Benny McCoy, Paris

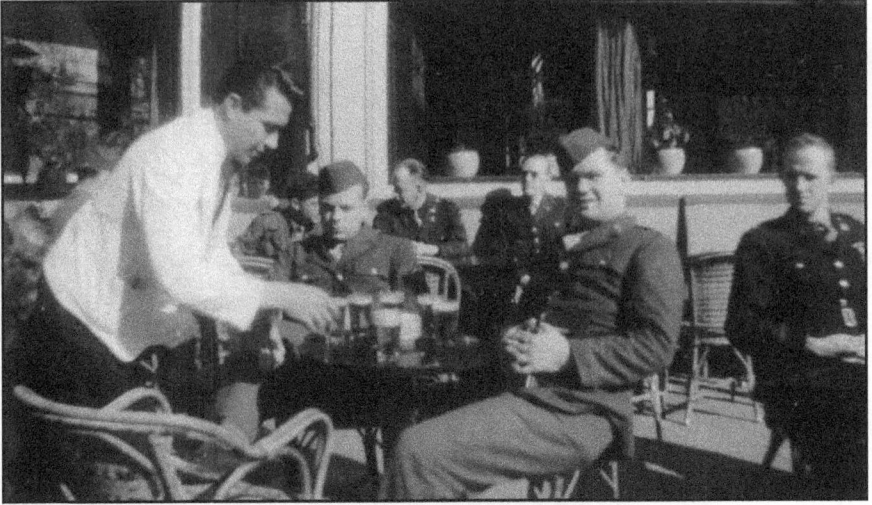

Benny McCoy and Hans Halverson, Paris

Benny McCoy, Paris

Victory Day in Paris; photo taken by Benny McCoy from OSS Paris office

Benny McCoy, Paris

Benny McCoy, Hans Halverson, Tommy Lowndes

Chapter 12

BATTLE OF THE BULGE, DECEMBER, 1944

ॐ

Benny McCoy and stepbrother Burtis Wall

FRANCIS KNAPP

WHEN THE GERMANS hit Paris, it was close to Christmas. They came right down the Champs.

BENNY MCCOY

The Germans hit Paris with a bombing raid. I'd been up all night and on duty sixteen hours. I had come in and was in a stupor. I just fell into my straw mattress. My duffel bag was looped around my arm. When I went to bed, I put the lock on my duffel bag and my arm in the loop of the bag to prevent anyone from waking me and taking my valuables. I always locked the bag to my bed when I went to work.

Francis started shaking me. He had on all his paraphernalia. He said, "McCoy, they're trying to get us. Get up. Let's go. I'm going to the air raid shelter."

I got up and staggered around there a little bit. They dropped a couple of bombs. I thought, *They'll get me before I ever make it to the air raid shelter.* I went back to bed.

During the Battle of the Bulge in the Ardennes forest, the weather was freezing and miserable. My stepbrother Burtis Wall was a medic who assisted a doctor in the Bulge. Burtis said there were several ambulances, and the doctor told him to take over for him and get the wounded into ambulances and to the hospital. During all the chaos of trying to help injured soldiers, Burtis remembered Patton making angry remarks while he led the soldiers in the Bulge.

When the Battle of the Bulge was in progress and the Germans had the greater armed force and thought they could annihilate the Americans, the German General at Bastogne demanded surrender. The 101st Airborne Division General McAuliffe answered: "Nuts." The German General, confused, asked the meaning of the word, whether that was affirmative or negative. I remember it well; it came out in the *Stars and the Stripes*.

One goof-up by military intelligence was the Battle of the Bulge. If we had been on our toes and the French underground had been on their toes, the Battle of the Bulge never would have happened because they would have headed it off before the German forces got back there.

What the Germans were doing was making out like they were bivouacking and that they were moving as many forces out of that pocket as they were moving into it. When they would move out of the pocket, they would stretch out so they would not be in close order. They were counting

102

the same number of troops going both ways—which was a lie. They were moving twice as many in that pocket as they were moving out, and so when they hit us, we didn't know where they were getting the troops. We later found out that they had been staging this. Hitler had been getting ready for it because he thought he could make a drive all the way to Antwerp. Hitler could have gotten all the way back behind us and still would have had a chance at winning the war. Eisenhower told Patton, "Turn your forces to the north, and get to the Battle of the Bulge."

LLOYD POSTEL

My wife, Vera, suggested one day after the war that we invite my partner, Roger, and my secretary's husband, Helmut, for dinner. The invitation was made, and the two men came for dinner. Helmut and Inge had moved from Germany to America. My secretary, Inge, had returned there for a visit. Roger's wife and children were visiting family in New York.

We were having martinis before dinner, and the war stories started. Helmut had been in the crew of a German 88 battery, first doing antiaircraft on the Mediterranean Coast and later using it against infantry in the Battle of the Bulge. He described one little valley with precise German detail, how high the steeple was and where it was located in relation to the stream and the trees. He told us how they had "ranged" the gun, using a tree or rock as a landmark to which they knew the exact distance; and they had done this with German precision.

My partner, who had been in Patton's Third Army, was listening, fascinated, and suddenly yelled, "Stemming!"

Helmut looked at him and said, "Ya, Stemming!"

My partner and Helmut recognized "Stemming" as a certain place of battle that they had both fought at.

Roger said, "You—you were pointing that gun at me!" Roger grabbed Helmut's glass and gave him another drink, and the evening went on.

Helmut and Vera couldn't get over how forgiving Americans can be, even when the war became that personal. We also told Helmut how inefficient and sloppy the American army was and how much better the Germans ran things.

Helmut's response was, "You think so? Have you ever tried to ram a 95 millimeter shell into an 88 millimeter breach?" We thought giving you the wrong ammunition for the weapon had been an American exclusive!

Chapter 13
LLOYD AND DON AND ITALY

❧

Don Brunette and Lloyd Postel

LLOYD POSTEL

IN NOVEMBER, 1944, I climbed onto the troop ship in Liverpool to go to
Naples. The backpack outweighed me by four pounds. My friend Kapitan
would push it in the back, helping me to get it up.

When our troop ship reached Naples, there were no port facilities left, but there was a big, sunken ship lying on its side with the bow on the beach. They had removed the superstructure above its main deck, so our ship pulled up to the main deck of this one. We climbed off onto the starboard hull of the sunken one and walked down the bow to the beach.

Don Brunette had a cousin, near Bari, I think, and he wanted to find a telephone. He began running up and down the beach yelling at the Italians he saw but didn't know enough of the language to get his message across. Then one of our guys yelled at him, pointing to a booth almost next to him that said "TELEFONO" across the top. He never did make the call.

Caserta was an out-of-the-way place close to the Red Sea. I didn't like that part. It's been decades since I've thought of some of these things. It's a city in southern Italy, about midway between Naples and Monta Casina, site of the biggest battle of the Italian campaign. Caserta was the Allied Force headquarters. Nearby in Santa Lucia was a huge palace that was occupied by General Clark from the American Fifth Army, General Alexander from the British Eighth, and a man from the Swiss armies. The palace resembled Versailles in France and had been the residence of the monarch of the kingdom of the two Sicilys in earlier days. It was the home of Napoleon's brother after Napoleon conquered Italy and set up his brother as the king. The OSS took over the castle, and our message center and the headquarters were inside it. The officers also lived there. The troops lived in the basement of a silk factory at the bottom of the hill and "commuted" to work on the back of a truck.

I went to Florence for a month and a half or so right at the end of the war. Field Marshal Albert Kesselring had already given up, and the OSS was trying a teletype machine code. They had one on the back of the truck. It was kind of a hut and was also airproof if you closed the door. Then Don and I had to ride in this thing while going up the Appian Way. We were going to set it up in the courtyard of this villa on a hillside above Rome.

I remember a lieutenant who had the misfortune of killing a friendly agent by accident. The agent was dropped at night, and the lieutenant met this guy, blasted away, and killed the agent. The lieutenant was in charge of the motor pool.

Some genius got the idea of seeing if we could make a teletype mobile, so we were sent up to Florence. The officers became nervous. They were all running every which way to get out of helping us. The officers in our unit were sure the mobile teletype system wouldn't work, and they were nervous.

It was like dropping a fox into a chicken yard—all the officers were ducking and weaving to avoid becoming involved. Then someone looked at Christianson, the lieutenant who had shot the agent, and suggested, "Send Christianson. He's through anyway." And so they yanked him out of the motor pool and sent him north with the teletype truck—and six idiots. Four idiots, who had stripes (sergeants), knew construction and electricity, and I carried and fetched while they put the aerials up and got everything ready. Then the lieutenant and sergeants looked at each other and asked, "What now?"

When we told them we were operators and could work the thing, Lieutenant Christianson didn't want to believe it at first. He asked, "You can work this thing?"

"Yes," we said. We sent his message to Caserta, coded and by radio.

About two days later, a message came back to Caserta saying, "General Clark is fascinated—test run." The general also sent a message to our lieutenant congratulating him on "the achievement."

Christianson's gratitude knew almost no bounds. He let Don and me use his jeep, and I taught Don to drive, partly, over Ponte Vecchio, the famous fourteenth century bridge. It was the only bridge in Florence that wasn't destroyed by the Germans.

PART 3

BACK TO THE HOME FRONT

INTRODUCTION

AT THE END of the war, while the OSS was coming to an end, an offer was made to Dad, one that promised a future in the organization that would become the CIA. He was brought back to Washington, D.C., for the sole purpose of working in the OSS, but he said, "Harry Truman did not see the necessity of extending the OSS. He downplayed it and let it die." In *Alliance of Enemies: The Untold Story of the Secret American and German Collaboration to End World War II*, Agostino von Hassell and Sigrid MacRae indicate that Harry Truman was convinced by J. Edgar Hoover to end the OSS. Furthermore, Truman had not worked closely with Donovan as Roosevelt had. "On September 20, 1945, Truman signed the order terminating the OSS."[8]

After the war ended, Dad and his OSS friends went back to the home front—to Washington D.C., to their hometowns, and to their families. In the following chapters, Dad and the OSS men he has kept in touch with since the war relate their journeys in life after their return from Europe.

Chapter 14

HOME FROM ITALY

🔊

Lloyd Postel and his wife in Poundon

LLOYD POSTEL

THE DAY I came home from the war was Friday the Thirteenth, but I never thought of it as a bad day. I came home on a slow boat, a liberty ship. We only had fourteen soldiers on it. When I came home, I finished another semester at junior college. Because they made funny rules for veterans at the time, I was able to count my time in the Army in Wisconsin for, I guess, a year. One way or another, I received three years' credit out of it, entered law school out of junior college, and then started practicing in San Francisco. If you ever want to try a social shock, junior college to law school is quite a leap.

THE G.I. BILL

The G.I. Bill was a very enlightened maneuver. I was a lawyer on the G.I. Bill; otherwise, I wouldn't have been. You didn't exactly roll in luxury with the

G.I. Bill, but at least it got you there. If you were willing to make a little sacrifice yourself, you could use it and get through school.

When I met Vera, she was a secretary in an insurance company for a fellow named Phil Rowland, with whom I had attended high school. I ran into Phil one day in San Francisco. He said, "Do you want some cases?" Everybody always said that. It was right after the war.

"Oh, yeah, fine, Phil, thanks," I said.

Well, a couple of days later, here came the invoice, and he meant it. So I became one of the company's lawyers.

I used to tease Vera. She had an accent you could slice with a knife. "This is Mr. Rowland's office," she'd say.

"Who?" I'd say.

She would answer, "Mr. Rowland's."

I would ask, "What's his first name?"

"Oh, it's you," she'd say.

One thing led to another. We would take her to lunch sometimes. I would try to get a date, and it was like running into a wall. One day Phil and I were sitting there "yakking" at his desk in the office with everybody else. I don't remember the conversation, but he said something like, "Well, you'll get married and have kids one day. Then you'll understand."

I left, and Phil told me later that she asked, "He's not married?"

When Vera and I were married, we got an apartment on Russian Hill in San Francisco for about two years. Then we bought a little house in Mill Valley.

Vera and I took one of our trips to a place we call "Lake Constance." The Germans call it "the Bodensee." It's a lake between Germany and Switzerland. On our way back, since we were close, I wanted to see Bausenlott, which was the name of the town where my mother's mother came from. It's a little farming community. When she left, I'm sure it was only a few hundred people. Now it's about 15,000. We found the city hall and the name Walther on monuments on the town square for the German kids that were killed in the two wars. Walther was my grandmother's maiden name.

We had this Volkswagen bus parked at the curb in front of a residence that was only a few doors down from the city hall. It was a farm home at one time and was surrounded by a fence. We stopped to talk to some people who were working in the driveway about a hundred feet back from the street. Vera could speak German, and she explained to them why we were there. We thanked them for their information and went back to the bus.

We were about to turn the key when they came running around the corner—a lady with her husband and an elderly man behind them. They came up to the window. The lady said to Vera, "This is my father (he was eighty-something), and he remembers the day that the two girls [my grandmother and my great aunt] left us to go to America." This was a little thing that we wouldn't forget from that trip. However, I didn't have any connection with the people there. I do more now with Vera's family than I ever did with mine. So it was a "nothing item" that I was a German American, and I think that the FBI readily agreed.

I'm retired, and I don't do much legal work now. I do a little with part-time depositions and motions for Dave Leach, the senior partner in the law firm. Four or five decades ago, he was the first employee my partner and I hired. So now we've gone the full circle, and I'm working for him. I don't try cases anymore. I have no clients. I don't care if the secretaries get along—I have none of those problems. Actually, I still struggle to get everything accomplished because I've slowed down so much. I get up at 8:00 in the morning with nothing to do, and I can't get it done by 5:00!

In 1999, Vera passed away. I was helping her back to bed. While I was taking her walker around the end of the bed, she fell on it. I said, "No, no, Toughie, you got to get up at the other end, up by the pillow," but she was already dead.

A RETURN VISIT TO POUNDON

I went back to Poundon Hill once. There was a radio station there. Vera and I took a train up to Oxford from London. I wanted to rent a car, but it wasn't available. They had a limousine and a tour guide available, though. *Fine,* I thought, *I'm here; let's go.* We went back to the valley, eight miles from Oxford. This guy who had been in Oxford for eight years was a tour operator and had never even heard of where Poundon was. It wasn't all that big, but it wasn't all that far. First thing we found was Bicester. One thing Bicester had was a movie house.

Kapitan, one of our friends at Poundon, got married while we were there in the war. At the wedding, he was holding a rifle. Rifles were crossed, and the bride and groom walked beneath them on Launton Road. Vera and I went down that same road, Launton. There was a little town between Bicester and Poundon. Then there it was—up on the hill, right where it should have been, with a chain-link fence around it and the towers. The driver whipped the limousine around, screeching to a halt in the gravel. We all bailed out and started running for the gate. These two English cops came around the other way and said, "No, no, no. You can't come in here."

It turned out that it was still secret, and it was still a radio station. What was secret about it wasn't evident. They weren't doing spy work anymore. It was something like their stage of B.B.C or something else, or whoever was their competitor.

The guy who was driving the car was explaining about me to the cops. They were fascinated, but that didn't make any difference. The cops said, "You aren't coming here. Never mind that you used to work here."

Poundon, by rumor, had a population of seventeen souls when we were there, so we're talking about small.

DON BRUNETTE

After the war, I went back to New York and completed my college work. I majored in accounting and taxes and worked at it for a couple of years. I found it dull, then changed to teaching. I taught in high school for a couple of years and loved it, but there was no money in it at the time. Then I became a salesman for Campbell Soup for a short period, until an opportunity came along to go into business with my brother in the hosiery business. Over the years, we did quite well. We were wholesalers and covered most of the Eastern Seaboard and Puerto Rico. We were in business for approximately thirty-five years.

In 1954, I married my wonderful wife, and I fathered three boys: Douglas, Jay, and David. Doug is a physician and is head of the emergency department at Hennepin Hospital in Minneapolis and also teaches at the Medical School at the University of Minnesota. Jay is also a physician and practices in Cartersville, Georgia, forty-five miles northwest of Atlanta. David followed his brothers and became a physician too. He is a child psychiatrist and practices in Smyrna, Georgia, near Atlanta.

Doug has two children; Jay has four; and David has two. Of Jay's four, three are triplets.

116

Chapter 15

HANS HALVERSON LEAVES FRANCE FOR NORTH DAKOTA

❧

House Hans Halverson built when he returned from the war

HANS HALVERSON

A SHORT TIME after I met Glenn Miller, I was released from the service. I went back to Fargo, North Dakota, and began a normal life. I had not been home and working long before my father told me I should build a house. He said that with things as cheap as they were, house prices would be going up and that this was a good time. I did what he said and first found a lot that I had to pay $600 to get. I then went to a lumber yard to ask about a contractor I could contact. I was given the name of Olaf Anderson, whom I called. He asked me to come out to his home to talk about a house.

There, in the kitchen, I saw this pretty girl who he told me was his daughter, and he called her in to meet me. The next day, I called her for a date, and six months later, we were married and moved into our new home. We have now had sixty-three years of a wonderful married life.

The first ten years of our marriage, I worked for a Pontiac dealer in Fargo. I then bought a small Ford and Mercury dealership in a small town close to Fargo but stayed there only two years, as a friend of mine had just started a car auction and wanted me to join him. For twenty years we were partners. Then I sold my share and went into the developing and building business in 1979. I joined with Haug Construction Company, and together we built condos, apartment houses, and houses. This went on for several years, until I decided that I should go on my own and slow down. I ended up with a sixty-two unit retirement home, a hotel, and several apartment buildings.

LaVerne and I have three children—two boys and a girl. Steve, our eldest, worked for Wells Fargo Trust but decided to start his own private trust company, and he is doing very well. Steve and Kay have three children—two boys and a girl, all married. Patti, our daughter, just moved back to Fargo, as her husband retired as a colonel in the Air Force after thirty years. They have two boys who are not married. Our third child, John Douglas, is married and has three boys, none of them married. LaVerne and I have five great-grandchildren.

My son Doug works with me, or I should say, I now work for him. He takes care of our properties, and all I do is go to the office each morning about 9:30 A.M. and go home about 2:00 P.M. I am now what they call a "gopher"—go for this and go for that

LaVerne Halverson, Angela McCoy Horn, Hans Halverson
at the Halverson lake house

Hans and LaVerne Halverson in Arizona

Chapter 16

BENNY AND FRANCIS RETURN TO WASHINGTON

&

BENNY MCCOY

MY JOURNEY HOME began in early in September of 1945. "One man out of the department will get to go home," I overheard an officer tell a supervisor. I had more points than the others in my OSS group. When I applied to come home first, that officer said, "I'll put your name on the top of the list."

My rating was a Number 5 Technician. I had good income—income like I never expected to make. I was offered a direct commission when I was coming home from Europe if I would stay for the Occupation for twelve more months. I said, "No, I'm not interested in staying
in Europe another year."

Early in September, I left Paris and went to Le Havre, France, on the English Channel to wait for my ship. Unfortunately, the ship was slow. The ship took at least three weeks

Benny McCoy

to arrive at Le Havre. I didn't have any duty and could come and go as I pleased. While I waited on the ship, I explored Le Havre. On September 5, 1944, there had been intensive bombing of German dock installations and military strong points at Le Havre. The bombs started a firestorm, and 2,500

French civilians died. On September 12, the German garrison in Le Havre surrendered.

When it was time for me to ship out from Europe, I looked at what all I had to sell. We were not allowed to change any more than $500. I gathered up everything that wasn't requisitioned and sold it. I came up with $1,200.

One guy never had any money and was always in some kind of a deal. He stayed at a chalet where several motorcycles were kept. This guy never had a dime. He received orders to ship out when I did. I knew he didn't have any money. When it was time for him to change his money, he was told he could only have $500.

He told me, "I haven't got a franc, not one."

I asked, "Do you want to make a hundred francs?"

"Yeah," he said.

"Take this $500, then give it back to me after we get through."

He said, "I'll do it," and he exchanged $500 for me. I gave him the hundred francs.

When we got on the ship, he asked, "How about letting me borrow some money?"

"I can't let you borrow some money, boy. I'm not ever going to see you again," I said.

"No, I'll pay it back. Just let me borrow $100."

I had about $1,250. I let him borrow about $100, and he started gambling. He made $1,000 and paid me back.

"Look," I said. "Go put that money in the ship's safe, and let the captain take care of it, or you're going to be broke."

So he did. We were out on the water eighteen days. He let the money stay there a week, and then he went for a haircut. When we got off the ship, he didn't have a cent. He came to me again, wanting to borrow some more money.

"No. I know where the Red Cross Club is. If you'll go down to the Red Cross Club, they'll give you a ticket home free." He followed the advice and was given a ticket.

My ship landed in Newport News, Virginia, on October 18, 1945. The soldiers were given free postcards there. I sent Myrl a postcard, letting her know that I was arriving in Washington, D.C. I stayed in Fort Henry, Virginia, for two or three days and then was sent to Washington, D.C., in an OSS area. I arrived in Washington, D.C., about October 21 and stayed about a week. I was told that it would be about two weeks before I could go home. The Army bought me a round-trip ticket for a forty-five-day rest.

In Washington, I boarded a train, and it took me three days to get to Lufkin, Texas. I boarded the train the evening of October 26 and arrived in Lufkin on October 29. For the first part of my trip, they put me in a Pullman, which had a bed. I arrived in New Orleans Friday night, and in Beaumont, Texas, about midnight Saturday but couldn't get a train out of Beaumont. I went to the bus station and asked an attendant where I could stay. He told me about a boarding house across the street. He said the bus would leave at 6:00 the next morning.

The train and the bus could only travel at thirty-five miles per hour because gasoline was so scarce. It took six hours for the bus to get to Huntington, Texas, from Beaumont. (Now it takes less than two hours to drive from Beaumont to Huntington.) Once I reached Huntington, I left my bags at the station and walked down to my grandpa's house. A cousin, Edmond Russell, had come home from the war and owned a car. He drove up while I was at Grandpa's. He asked, "Have you seen Myrl?"

I said, "No, I just got in."

He asked, "Does she know you're here?"

I said, "No, but I sent her a card, letting her know I had arrived in Washington."

He said, "I've got to see this," and drove me to my wife's mother's house, where Myrl was staying. We drove right up to the back porch. My wife and her family were all eating in the parlor, which they used as a dining area. A preacher named Foxy Williams was preaching a revival in the community, Rocky Hill, and was eating with the family.

I got out of the car and started around between the car and the house. Somebody told Myrl I was there. She sailed off of the porch to meet me, knocking her niece Jo Ann off of the porch. While Myrl's sister grabbed Jo Ann, I reached up and caught Myrl before she hit the ground. In just a few minutes, everyone in Rocky Hill knew I was home. Suddenly, friends and relatives were coming over to see me.

I called my mother to tell her I was in Rocky Hill. She met me at the bus station the following Monday night in Lufkin. We visited awhile, and then she caught the next bus back home.

When I came home, I think I deposited $2,000 in the bank—the most money I'd ever seen or heard of in my life. Then I bought a car. The place where I purchased the car wouldn't cash my check. Therefore, I bought my first medical policy. I took out a policy with Omaha. They cashed the check, and I went back and paid $512 for the car. It had 27,000 miles on it.

Myrl went back to Washington with me. We rented an apartment a few blocks from the White House. When I returned to Washington, I got sick and stayed in the hospital for a month. When I was released from the hospital, Francis had returned to Washington from Europe. He visited us often at our apartment. We were all a long way from our families and enjoyed the company. Once, Myrl had forgotten to pick up an item at the commissary, where we bought groceries. I told her I'd go down to a little store. Francis had come over and he said, "No, I'll get it." He left and came back with an armload of groceries and wouldn't let me pay for them.

For Easter, 1946, Myrl and I received an invitation from President and Mrs. Truman to a picnic on the White House lawn. However, the event coincided with a thirty-day leave the OSS gave me before I continued with college at Georgetown. We went home to Texas for that leave. Francis followed us home. Cars were scarce, but Francis and I each bought a car. He bought a Lincoln, and I bought a '38 Plymouth. He preferred following me instead of having to deal with a map and directions. Myrl and I were going to Nacogdoches, Texas, and Francis was going home to Brownsville, Texas.

One day on the trip, we came to a detour at a railroad. Somehow Francis didn't see me turn. I turned around to go look for him. He had turned onto the property in front of the depot and driven by the railroad looking for me. So the third day, we continued the trip. We spent the night somewhere in Georgia, where we rented cabins.

On the fourth day, Francis said, "Benny, I'm going to drive in to Brownsville tonight."

I said, "There's no way."

He said, "If this thing (the Lincoln) holds together, I'm going to Brownsville tonight." He was tired and ready to be home, but he decided to continue the trip to Nacogdoches with us before going on further south to Brownsville. We had been driving through a big rainstorm, and we finally stopped at my mother's house in Nacogdoches. Later, Francis told me, "I don't see how I ever got back home without you."

When we returned home for a visit, my mother-in-law invited us to a revival at her church. We went with her to the revival. That's when my conscience got the best of me. The training I had received—including the signs that said "Learn to hate, and learn to kill"—had lasted for twenty weeks. The training had made me so angry that I had wanted to kill everybody coming down on my case. At the revival, I got rid of all that hostility.

OSS Changes

When I was discharged from the Army, I was hired again by the OSS, but as a civilian. During this time, OSS was changed to SSU (Strategic Services Unit) and was changed later to the CIA. The OSS debriefed me on what I would be facing and on the organization's expectations.

War Bonds

The government deducted war bonds from my salary but I couldn't find out where the money went when I asked for it. Suddenly, in 1949, I received a $300 check from the government. The correspondence didn't say what the check was for. I cashed it. I didn't say anything else about the war bonds. I quit arguing with them. I had been arguing with them since 1946. Around 1952, I received a check from them for $1,200. Again, nothing was said about what the check was for. I cashed it and didn't ask any questions.

The G.I. Bill and Education

After the war, the G.I. Bill paid all of my college expenses—that is, everything except the books. I received my degree from Stephen F. Austin University in Nacogdoches. Later, a company that I worked for sent me to Texas A & M every summer for a refresher course. The company paid the bill for me then. I'm about twenty-five to thirty credits from a doctorate degree.

The G.I. Bill enabled me to become an agricultural professional. As a graduate of SFA, I was qualified as a vocational agricultural teacher. The vocational program of agriculture was a state program. However, there was an additional program that added $1,400 annually per teacher that increased the salary of vocational agricultural teachers above that of ordinary teachers.

When I graduated, I found that there was more demand for agricultural experts with technical training in the production of beef and poultry than there was in teaching vocational agriculture in public schools. The salary for a feed salesman was at least double or triple the salary of a vocational agriculture teacher. At the time, I entered into the ministry, this job worked well for me because my family needed the income. Feed companies desired a person with my training to be on their staff and permitted me to continue to take other courses to further qualify myself in keeping poultry and livestock healthy.

Aside from going back to college after I returned to Texas, I worked for several years as a salesman for a company that manufactured and sold feed products for poultry and livestock. It also had a hatchery that hatched out baby chicks to sell. We had from two to four million chickens to feed, and I was poultry supervisor for the company over Texas and Louisiana. I was responsible for finding new feed dealers and new growers. We assisted our growers in finding financing to go into the poultry business, and we furnished technical help for profitable production. We were literally involved from the very beginning of whatever feed business we were dealing with, whether it was dairy cattle or beef cattle, horses, or poultry. As the poultry supervisor, I was involved in not only the sale of feed and baby chicks and laying hens but also in servicing many producers who were producing broilers for eggs. This involved helping the grower avoid disease in his flocks or herd and insuring a healthy profit for the grower or producer.

Eventually, I became a preacher and have pastored four churches in Texas. While pastoring churches, I have worked as a bookkeeper for a lumber company, built homes, and partnered in a used car dealership. My pastoral ministry demanded a great deal of my time, and I became involved in not only pastoring a local church but also in serving a number of years as a sectional secretary for the Youth Department in the Texas District of the United Pentecostal Church International (UPCI). After two or three years in this capacity, I was elected sectional president of the youth department. The next position I was given was sectional secretary for the ministry of that section. After five years in that position, I was elected district presbyter over that section. At that time, there were seven sections in Texas. While I was still presbyter, the sections were increased to thirteen. After being elected to six terms in this position, I resigned as district presbyter and transferred to another section.

During the course of my ministry, I also served about twenty-six years as a radio commissioner for the UPCI. I also served at least five years as a representative for campus evangelism in the south region of the United States. During that time, I was elected at a UPCI General Conference to serve as an executive presbyter on both the executive and general boards of the UPCI.

In 1977, I opened a Christian school, United Christian Academy (UCA), in my church. UCA has been highly successful and for many years has been among the elite gold model schools of the Accelerated Christian Education (ACE) organization. At the state, national, and international conventions, UCA has annually rated among the top-ranking schools in the receiving of awards. Many of our graduates have entered into the ministry. A great majority of our other students have continued in higher education.

126

Myrl and I had three children: Randall, Darrell, and Angela. After the boys were born, we lived in Lufkin, Texas, and Victoria, Texas. Later we moved to Nacogdoches, where Angela was born. For about six years, we drove thirty miles one way from Nacogdoches to Center, Texas, for every service at the church where I was a pastor. In 1960, we finally moved to Center to be closer to the church. In 1969, I became the pastor of First Pentecostal Church in Port Arthur, Texas. Myrl and I have lived in Port Arthur for over thirty-four years. We have been blessed with ten grandchildren and ten great-grandchildren.

UNINFORMED PEOPLE IN THE TWENTY-FIRST CENTURY

People are uninformed. Every major country in the world has to have a front line at peacetime. In the United States, the CIA is that front line. It doesn't mean that all of them are good guys. You will have a rotten egg every once in a while. When I was in the OSS, I wouldn't have sold anybody any information for any amount of money. We were so patriotic that if a man would have reneged on us and switched over to the enemy, he would have been in danger of someone killing him.

I live in the only county in Texas that went Democrat against President Bush—Jefferson County. Everything is unionized, all petrochemical. One day I was in the YMCA and heard some men talking. These guys were saying, "We need to do away with the Electoral College."

I walked to where they were and listened to them a minute or two. Most of them know me because I jog at the YMCA, and they know I'm a pastor. "Hey, why do you guys want to do away with the Electoral College? You want to do away with the states that only have four votes, states that don't have much population? And you want to take New York, Wilmington, Chicago, St. Louis, Houston, and Los Angeles and let them elect a president? Then all the states that only have maybe a million or two or three million people—you don't want to give them a vote? That's what the Electoral College is all about. That's why our founding fathers put it in, so that the small states would still have a voice. And you don't want them to have a voice? You just want a big bunch of people in the big cities to have a voice?"

One of them said, "Hey, I didn't know that."

We have many people who know so little about our government. You've got to speak up and be heard.

127

Cecil Morton wrote in a letter to me: "I heard about you being in the military and in France, and I wanted to write to you and tell you that I'm praying for you."

When I wrote him back, I thanked him for praying for me, for taking time to write me to let me know he was concerned about my life, and asked him to keep praying for me.

After the war, I saw a sign on my boss's desk that said, "A person that uses profanity when he talks does so because he doesn't have sense enough to express himself any other way." That was about the best I had ever seen it. That boss had another sign that said, "If you don't do more work than you get paid for, you may not get paid for more work than you do." Both of those signs made an impression on me.

In England, there was a pub right down the hill from where our station was. Guys I knew would go to the pub to drink, but I didn't go with them. I wasn't interested in drinking. The main thing I was interested in was staying alive and getting home before I died.

Three old boys got together, and they were going to go out one night on the town. One of the boys said, "Well, I can't go until I run by and see the priest, because if I get drunk tonight and something happens and I am killed, I'll go to hell. But if I go see the priest and have him pray for me, then I'll be OK."

Though I didn't drink at the pub with the guys, I was still looking for something from God. The first church I went to when I came home was Cecil Morton's church. When I met him, I shook hands with him and thanked him for the letter that he wrote. I remember the day that he led me to the banks of the Angelina River and baptized me in the name of Jesus Christ. My spirit had been hungry for God's Spirit all of my life, but I just hadn't found the right place to sit by the right gate at the right time.

The preacher who wrote me a letter had something different to offer me than anybody else ever did. Of all the preachers that stayed at our house, all the preachers that I gave my bed to, all the preachers that my folks fed, all the preachers that were their friends, not one of them wrote me a letter during my three years in the military. But one man that had never met me wrote me a letter and said, "I'm praying for you. I'm concerned about you."

Benny McCoy and niece Lajuan when he was home on leave

Benny and Myrl McCoy

Benny McCoy waiting to go home from the war

Benny McCoy waiting to go home from the war

Benny and Myrl McCoy

Myrl Mccoy in Washington, D.C.

Benny McCoy

Myrl McCoy

Benny McCoy (on the right) as salesman

United Pentecostal Church in Center, Texas,
where Rev. B. H. McCoy was pastor from 1954 to 1969

Christian Life Center (First Pentecostal Church, Port Arthur, Texas),
where Rev. B. H. McCoy has pastored since 1969

EPILOGUE

🙰

ANGELA HORN

OVER THIRTY YEARS ago, when I was engaged to be married, my future husband and I were planning to live in Houston, Texas. Until my wedding day arrived, I would drive to Houston to see my fiancé when he couldn't make the trip to my hometown in Port Arthur, Texas, to see me.

How well I remember my dad sitting down with me and instructing me on how to read the map of Houston with its north-south and east-west freeways and the city's Loop 610. He said, "If you'll just remember that Interstate 10 goes east and west, Interstate 59 and 45 go north and south, and 610 loops around Houston, you won't get lost." I never had a problem after that with finding my way around Houston. Sometimes I had to check my map for directions, but it wasn't difficult to find my way.

During the years it took me to write this book, I faced some roadblocks along the way. With roadblocks, most likely one is taken on a detour. Detours will direct you to your destination, just not the way you planned.

A couple of my computers crashed. That caused delays. Then I went to libraries. There I could do research and type.

I went back to college (to finally complete my degree as I promised Daddy I would). After working nights, going to college during the day, and studying in between with not nearly enough sleep, I had to delay the book yet again.

There were more roadblocks and more detours, but a desire persisted in me to complete this book to honor my dad, B. H. "Benny" McCoy; Francis Knapp; Hans Halverson; Lloyd Postel; Don Brunette; Al Clark; Arne Nilsen; and others who were so kind to share their stories. I was anxious to share these stories with others and knew I must press on.

Then I faced another roadblock. My mother, Archie Myrl Morehead McCoy, was diagnosed with cancer and died in March of 2008. Grief led me through that detour, and life has changed.

My mother-in-law, Fern Horn, had passed away in May of 2007. My mother and mother-in-law didn't have the opportunity to see the completion of this book, but they helped me to write the chapter "Home Front Memories."

Mother and Daddy were married almost sixty-five years. Daddy stays busy these days helping my brother Darrell McCoy in ministering to the church they pastor in Port Arthur, Texas. At eighty-six years of age, he continues a regimen of jogging, walking, and working out on fitness machines for exercise. He works on the farms in the family and practices his grandparenting skills—and reminisces about growing up on the farm, courting my mother, serving in World War II and the OSS, and sharing his life with Mother and my brothers and me.

As I think about the values passed to me from my parents, I am reminded of this verse: "Remove not the ancient landmark, which thy fathers have set" (Proverbs 22:28 KJV). I give honor to my parents for the love and values they gave me.

At this time, Francis Knapp still lives in South Texas and Dad in Southeast Texas. Lloyd Postel from California, Arne Nilsen from Norway, and Hans Halverson from North Dakota are no longer with us. I cherish the occasional phone calls with Lloyd, Hans and LaVerne, and Francis Knapp and am grateful for the correspondence with Arne. Each time I would call Hans and LaVerne, one would answer, and the other would pick up the other phone. The three of us would converse together just like I would with my own mother and daddy a lot of times when I would call them. Sweet memories.

Dad and I talk on the phone and visit as often as possible. He adores his family, and we adore him.

Al stayed married to his "blueblooded" love until his death. Don was also devoted to a lifetime of marriage and loved his wife as long as he lived.

All of the Phantom Seven shared these two things in common: love of family and lifetime marriage, two great qualities needed more than ever in the 21st century.

IN MEMORIAM: AL CLARK,
ONE OF THE PHANTOM SEVEN
Benny McCoy

After WWII, Al Clark applied for a commission as an officer in the Korean War and was accepted; he served in that war on a ship. After WWII, he married his "blueblood" love, Betty. They settled in the Detroit area and had two daughters.

I visited Al and his family once when I went to a church conference in Detroit and another time when Myrl and I visited there together with a minister friend and his wife. Al told his daughters, "You need to know these men. They are both ministers. You need to talk to them about who you're going to marry." He was teasing his daughters.

One time Al called me and said he was going on a trip to Mexico City and asked if he could borrow the little camera I had purchased when we worked in the OSS in Paris. The camera was a treasure, one that could not be replaced because of its history; but we had a strong bond of trust since working together in the OSS message center, so I loaned him the camera, and Al returned it after the trip.

This special recognition has been added in Al's memory because he was a close comrade to this group.

ENDNOTES

. Bonnie Angelo, *First Mothers* (New York: Perennial, 2001), 22–28.

. Kay Summersby Morgan, *Past Forgetting; My Love Affair With Dwight D. Eisenhower* (New York: Simon and Schuster, 1976), 282–283.

. Stephen Mansfield, *Never Give In, The Extraordinary Character of Winston Churchill* (Nashville, Tennessee: Cumberland House Publishing, Inc., 1995), 73.

. Stephen Mansfield, *Never Give In: The Extraordinary Character of Winston Churchill* (Nashville, Tennessee: Cumberland House Publishing, Inc., 1996), 139.

. Allen Dulles, *The Secret Surrender* (New York: Harper & Row Publishers, Incorporated, 1966), 4, 8–9.

. Ibid., 12.

. Kenneth Alford, *Treasure Stories of World War II* (Mason City, IA: Savas Publishing Company, 2000), chapter 11.

. *Alliance of Enemies: The Untold Story of Enemies: The Untold Story of the Secret American and German Collaboration to End World War II*, Agostino von Hassell and Sigrid MacRae (St. Martin's Griffin/Thomas Dunne books, 2008); Pages 292-294.

INDEX

A

Alexander, General, 109
Anderson, Olaf, 121
Angelo, Bonnie, 3
Austrian Crown Jewels, 97

B

Beneke, Tex, 86
Battle of the Bulge, 40, 105-107
Bombs, 32, 49, 59, 86, 90, 91, 106, 125,
British, 13, 50, 60, 70, 73, 78, 89-90, 110
Brunette, David, 120
Brunette, Don, ii, xi, xiv, 2, 29, 31-33, 50, 71, 109, 110, 111, 120, 139, 140
Brunette, Douglas, 120
Brunette, Jay, 120
Bruuen, Elsa, 57, 58
Bruuen, Petter, 57, 58

C

Cadogan Square, 32
California, 2, 28, 97, 140
Churchill, Winston, i, xii, 49, 51, 60, 97
CIA, 115, 129, 131
Clark, Al, xiv, 2, 35-36, 86, 89, 139, 141
Clark, General, 109
Cockney, 60

D

D-Day, 86
Decunia, Leonard, "Linny," 70
DeGaulle, General, 50

Denman, Leslie, 92
Donovan, William J., 52, 71, 88, 91, 115
Due, Dan, 37
Due, Jack, 37
Dulles, Allen, 52, 71

E

Eisenhower, Dwight, i, xi, 4, 50-51, 78, 91, 97, 107, 143
Eisenhower jackets, 93
England, 2, 13, 26, 32, 35, 49, 50-51, 55, 60, 70, 71, 72, 132
English Channel, 51, 86, 89-90, 125

F

Fort Knox, Kentucky, 10-11

G

General Clark, 110-111
Germany, 28, 50, 51, 54-55, 57, 59-60, 89-92, 107, 118
GI Bill, 118,129
Guidroz, Reverend V. Arlen, ii

H

Halvorson, Hans, xii, xiii, xiv, 1, 2, 25-26, 29, 35, 49, 50, 53, 70, 76, 83, 86, 93, 94, 95, 102, 104, 121, 123, 139, 140, 151, 153
Halvorson, John Douglas, 122
Halvorson, Patti, 122
Halvorson, Steve, 122
Halvorson, LaVerne, xiii, 49, 122, 123, 140
Henrikson, Todd, 95, 96
Hitler, Adolph, 49, 52, 54-55, 60, 90

143

Soldiers guarding tomb of Unknown Soldier on Veterans Day, 2008, Paris, France—photo taken by Louise Burkhartsmeier in 2008

Plaque on wall at entrance to Lido Club, Paris, France—photo taken by Louise Burkhartsmeier in 2008

Eiffel Tower, Paris, Prance—photo taken by
Louise Burkhartsmeier in 2008

LIDO CHAMPS-ELYSEES, Paris, France—photo taken by
Louise Burkhartsmeier in 2008

Benny and Myrl McCoy's 50th anniversary celebration

Hans Halvorson, Francis Knapp, Benny McCoy, and Lloyd Postel at
Brownsville, TX, for *Phantom Seven* interview

Lloyd Postel and Darrell McCoy at Tipotex Chevrolet, Brownsville, TX, *Phantom Seven* interview

Angie McCoy Horn and Benny McCoy at Tipotex Chevrolet, Brownsville, TX, *Phantom Seven* interview

Hans Halverson and Francis Knapp at Tipotex Chevrolet,
Brownsville, TX, *Phantom Seven* interview

Ted Poe and Dad

151

JoyLife Press

To order more books, contact us at:
joylifepress@gmail.com,
P.O. Box 956, Huntington, TX 75949,
or (909) 334-2564.